THE
GREY
GHOST

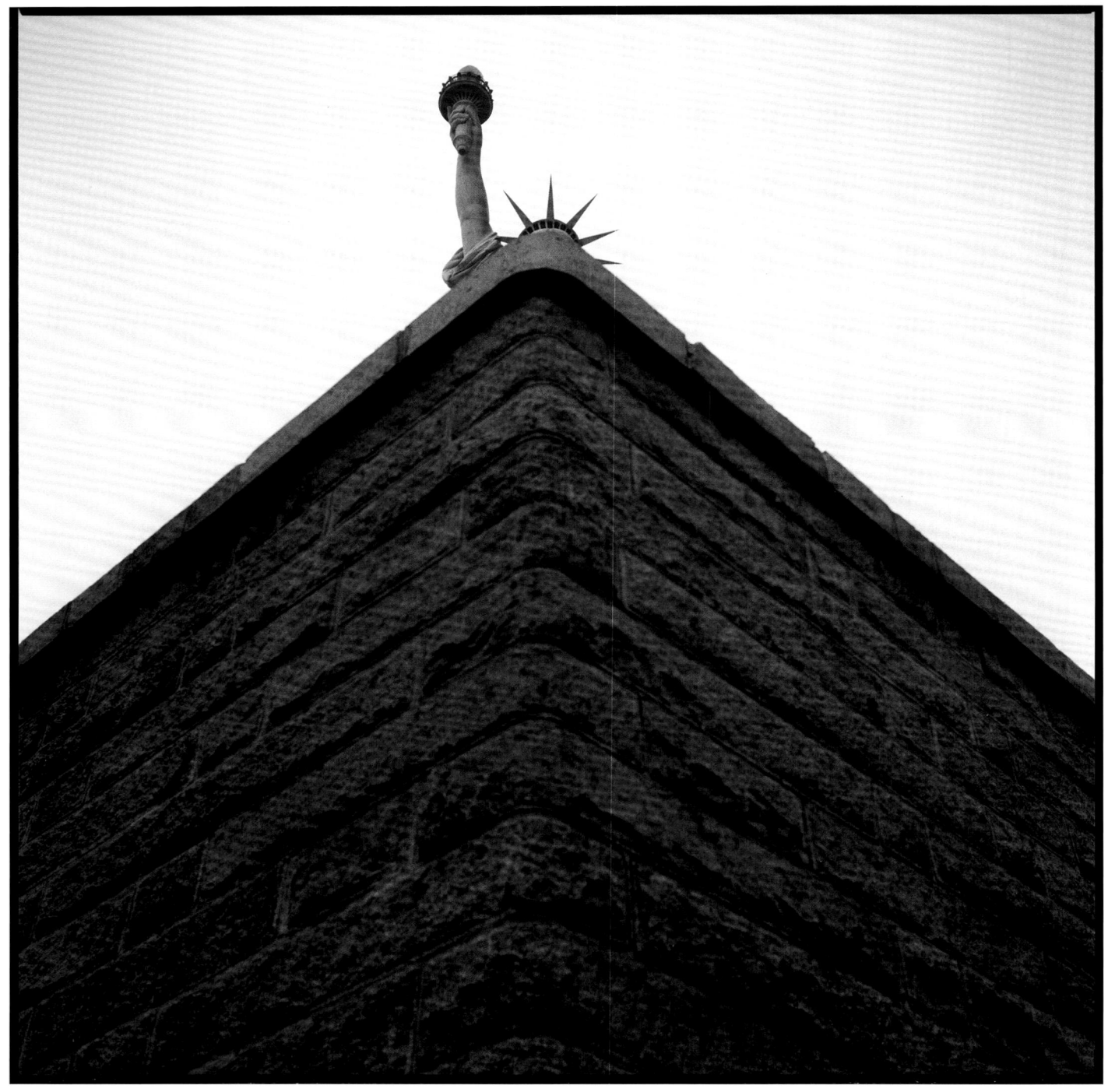

For Dylan

Sunken-eyed girl on Delancey Street
Bulletproof glass in the KFC
So keep the man safe in his paper hat
Keep the wrong hands off the biscuit fortune

Sunken-eyed girl don't let me go
You're the whole world and you barely know

FROM THE SONG "SUNKEN-EYED GIRL" BY MIKE DOUGHTY

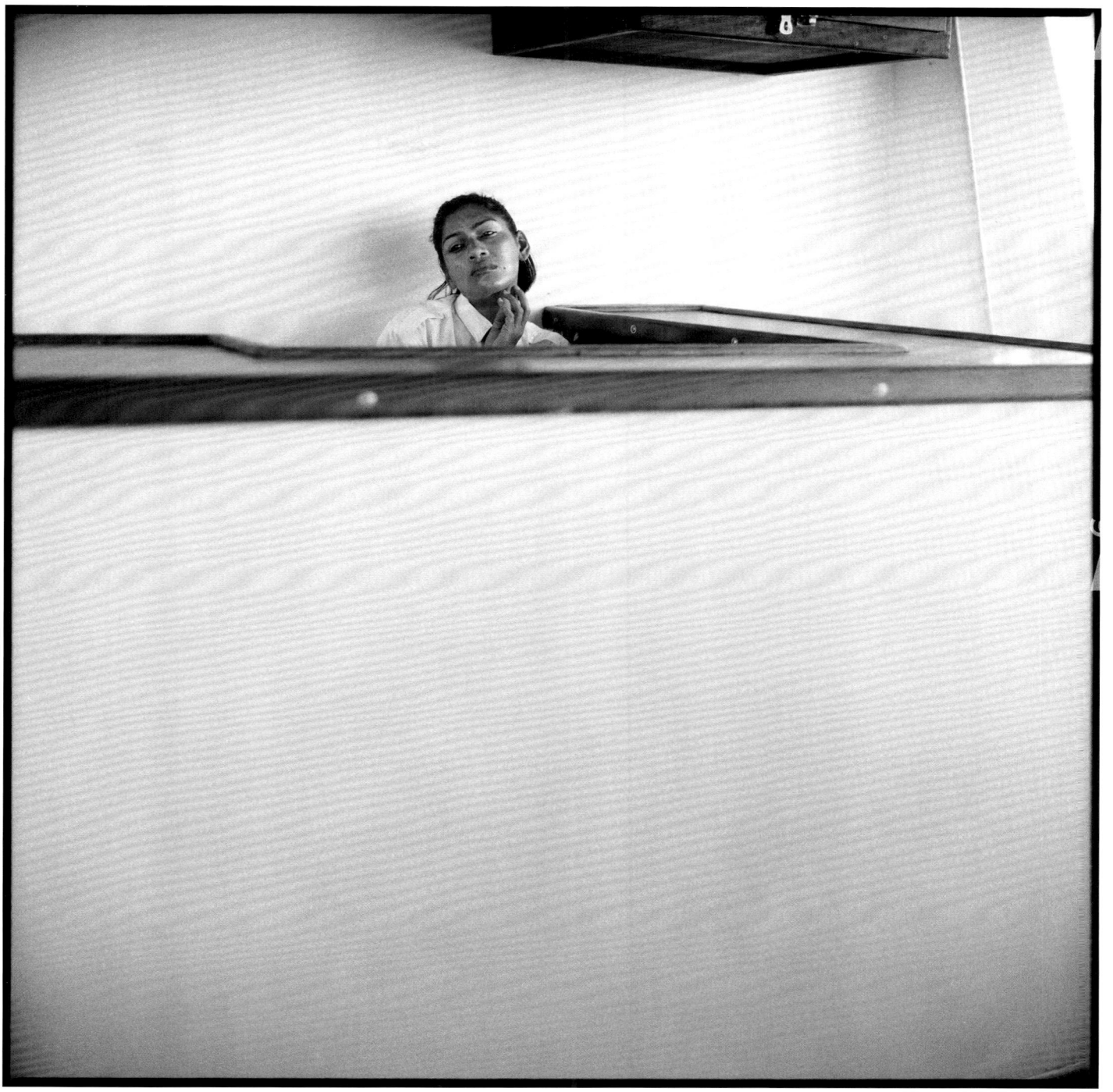

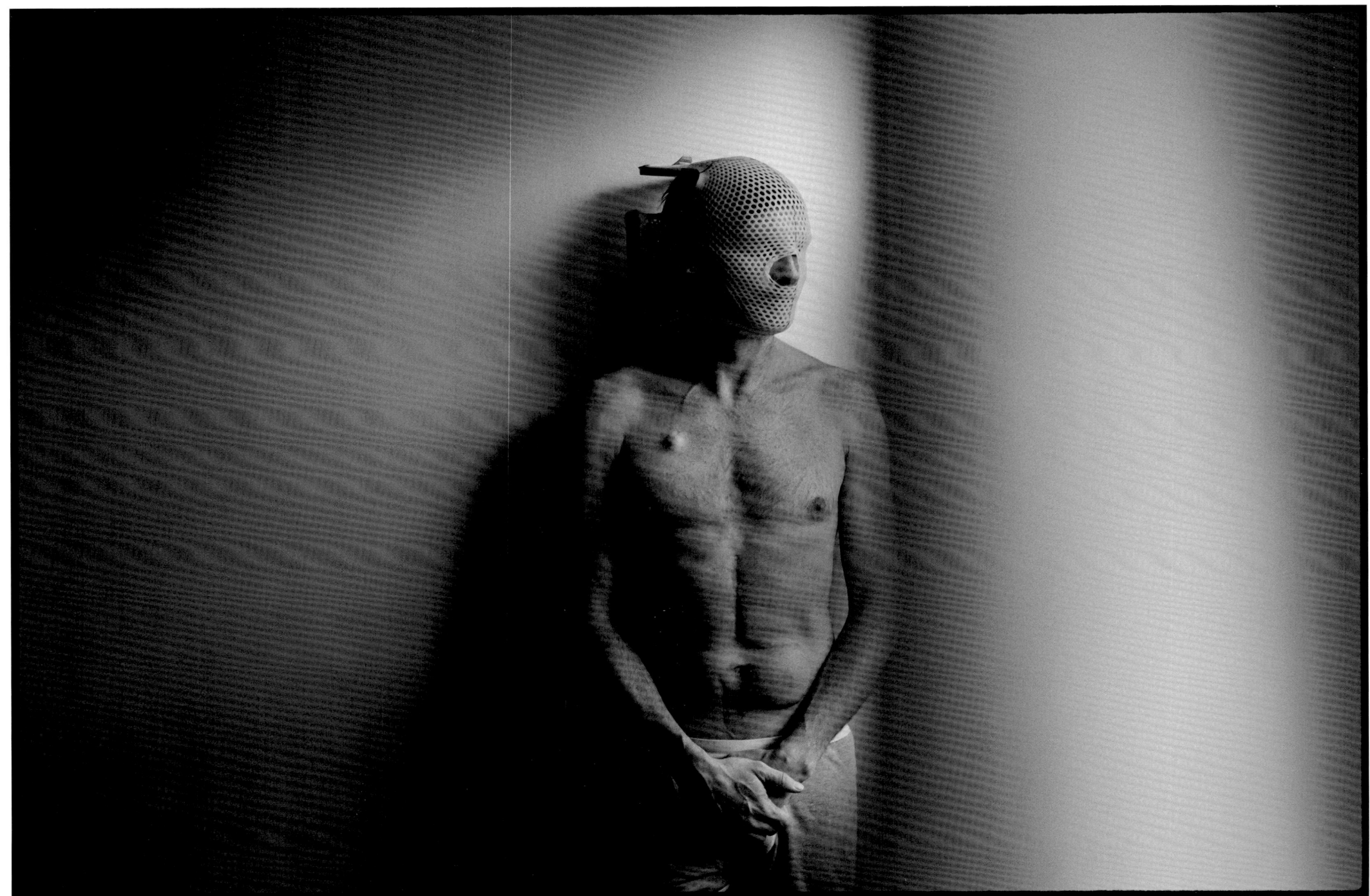

THE
GREY
GHOST

DAN WINTERS

ROCKY NOOK

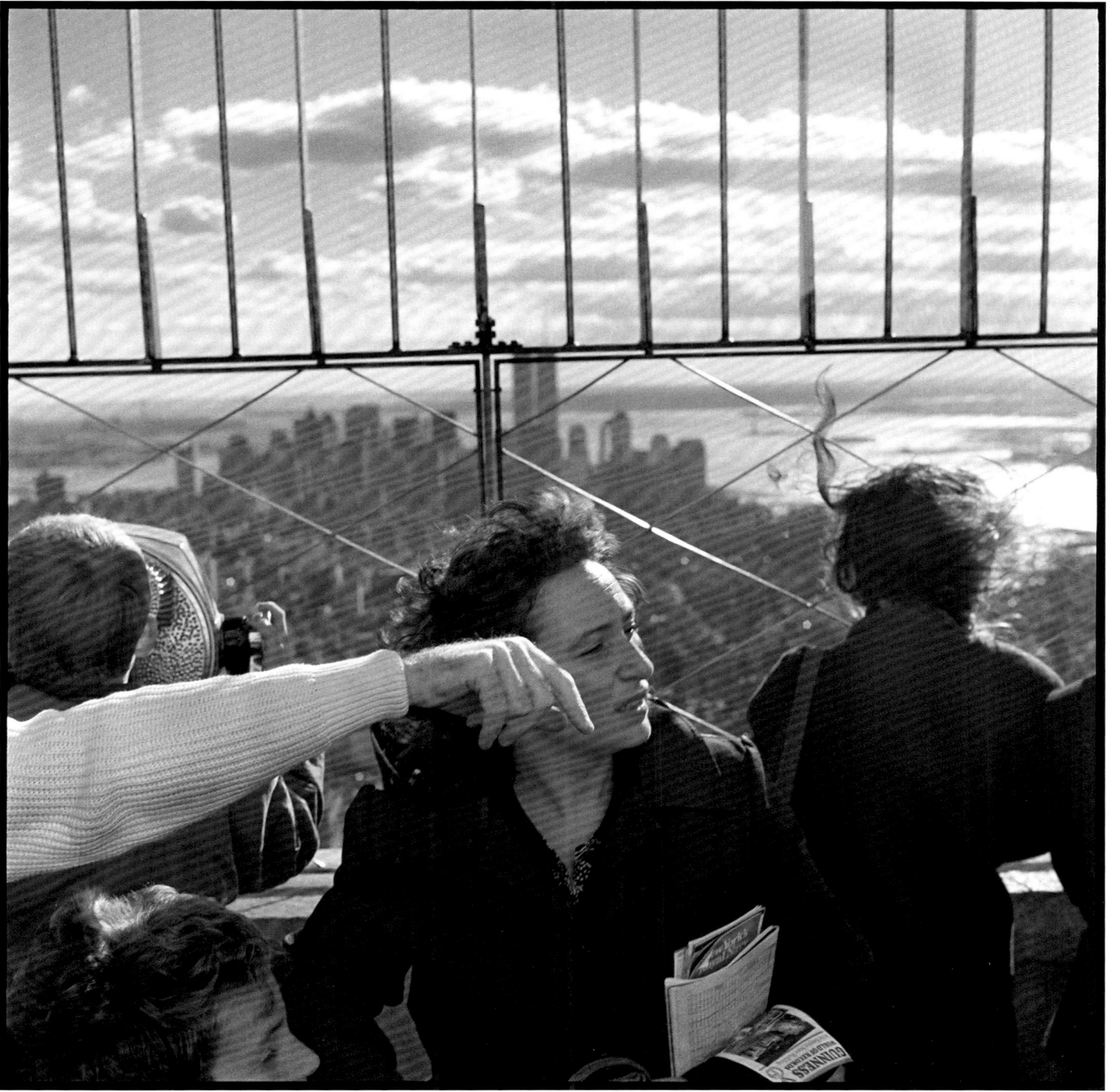

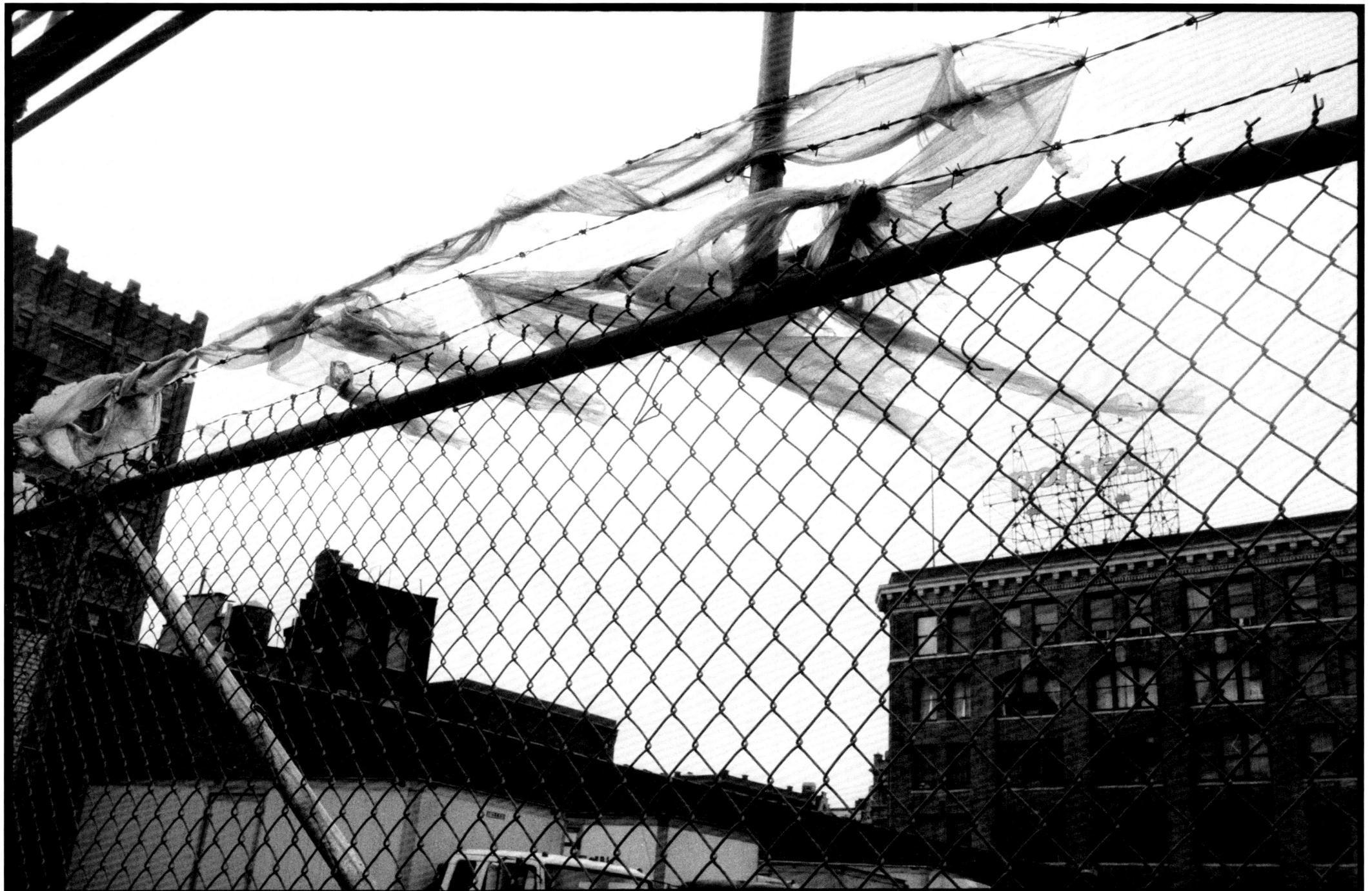

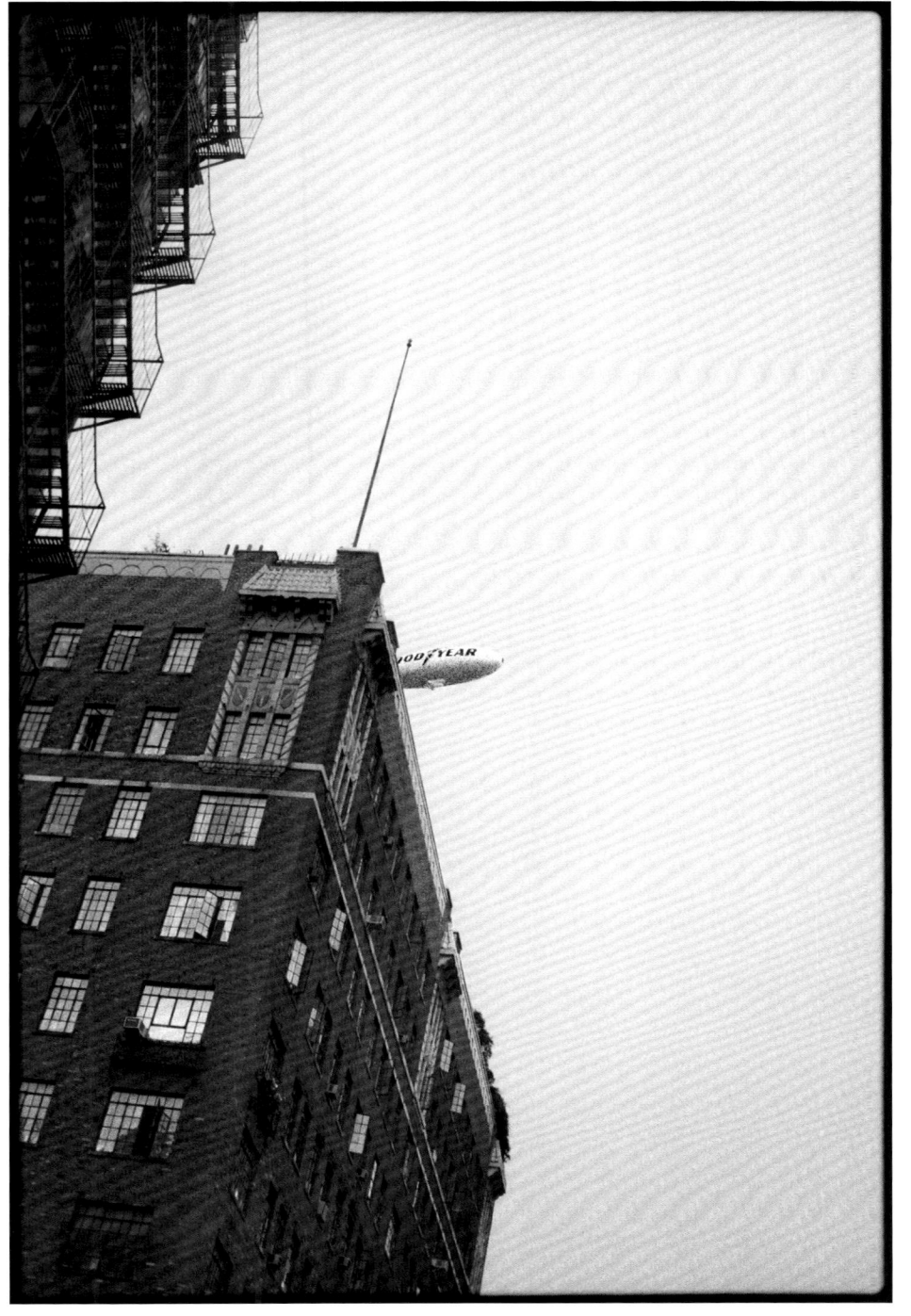

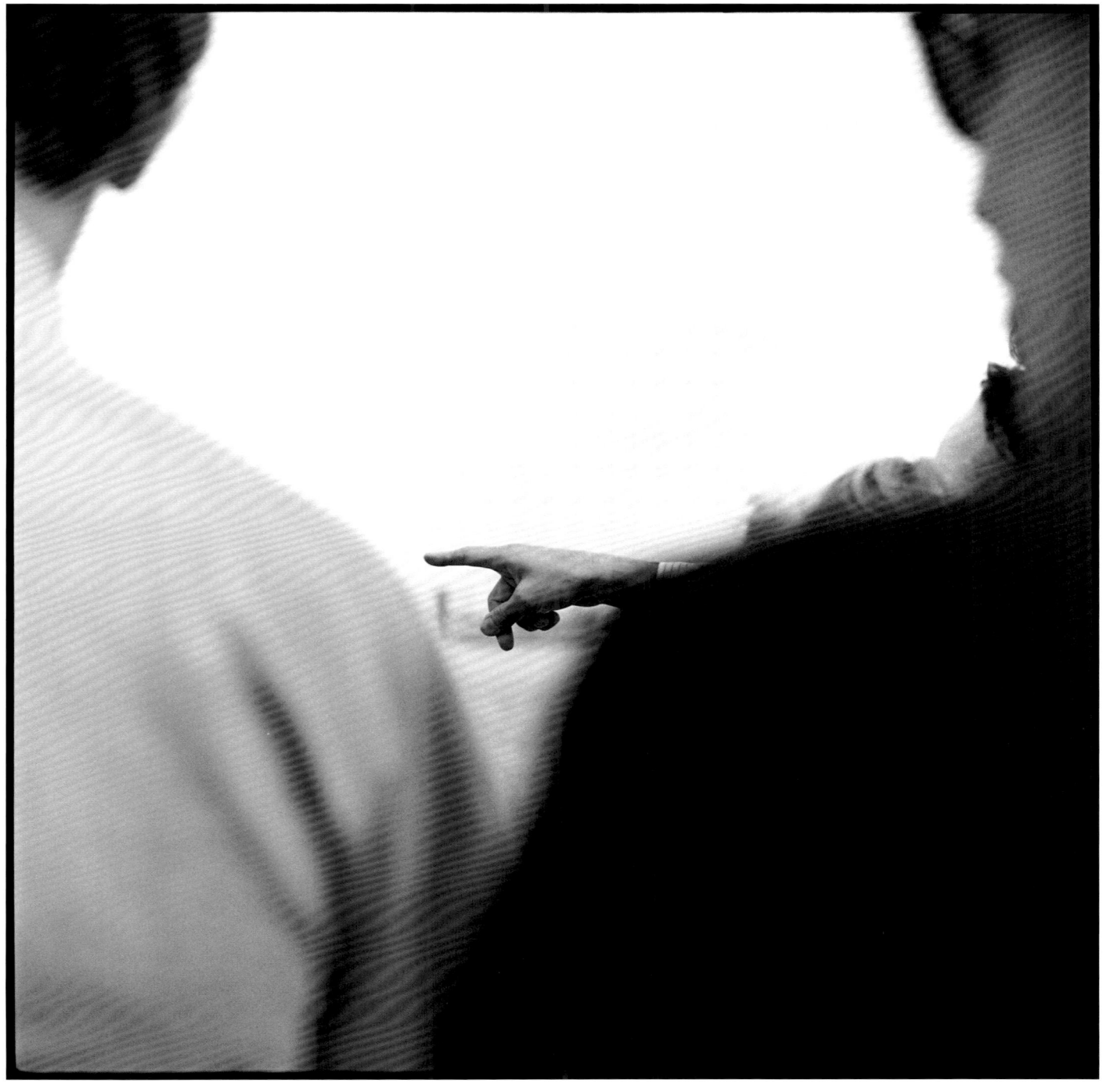

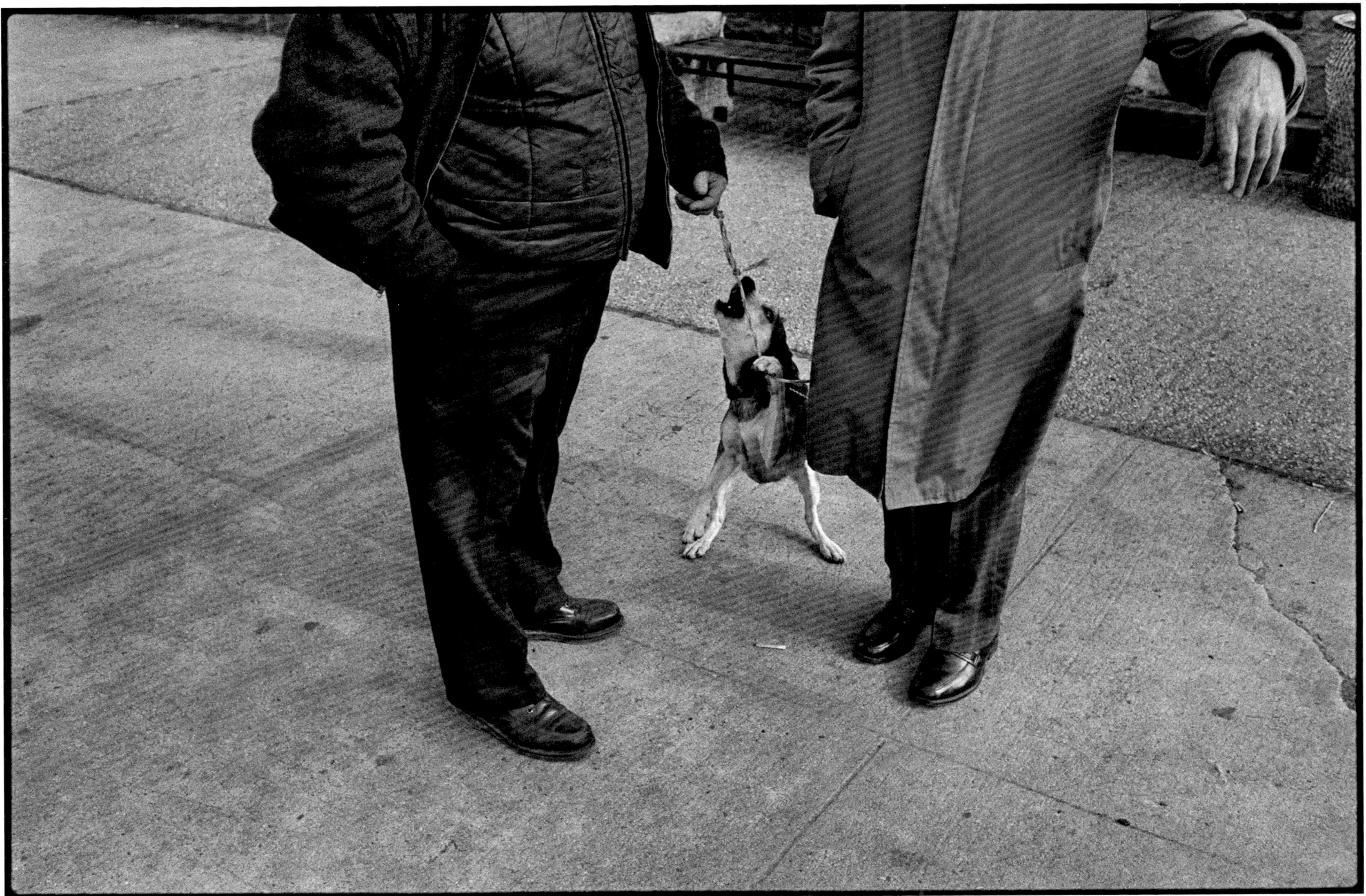

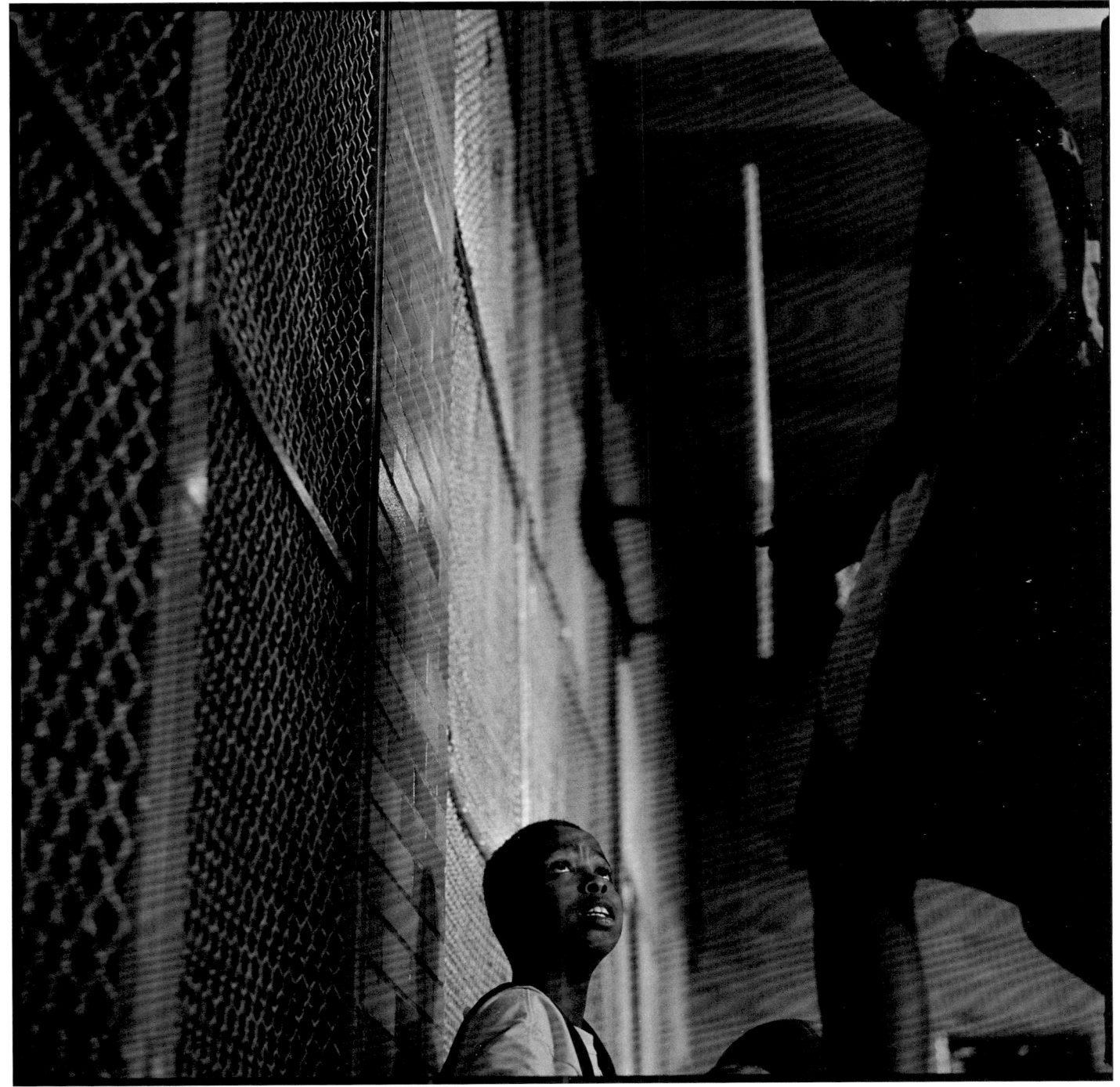

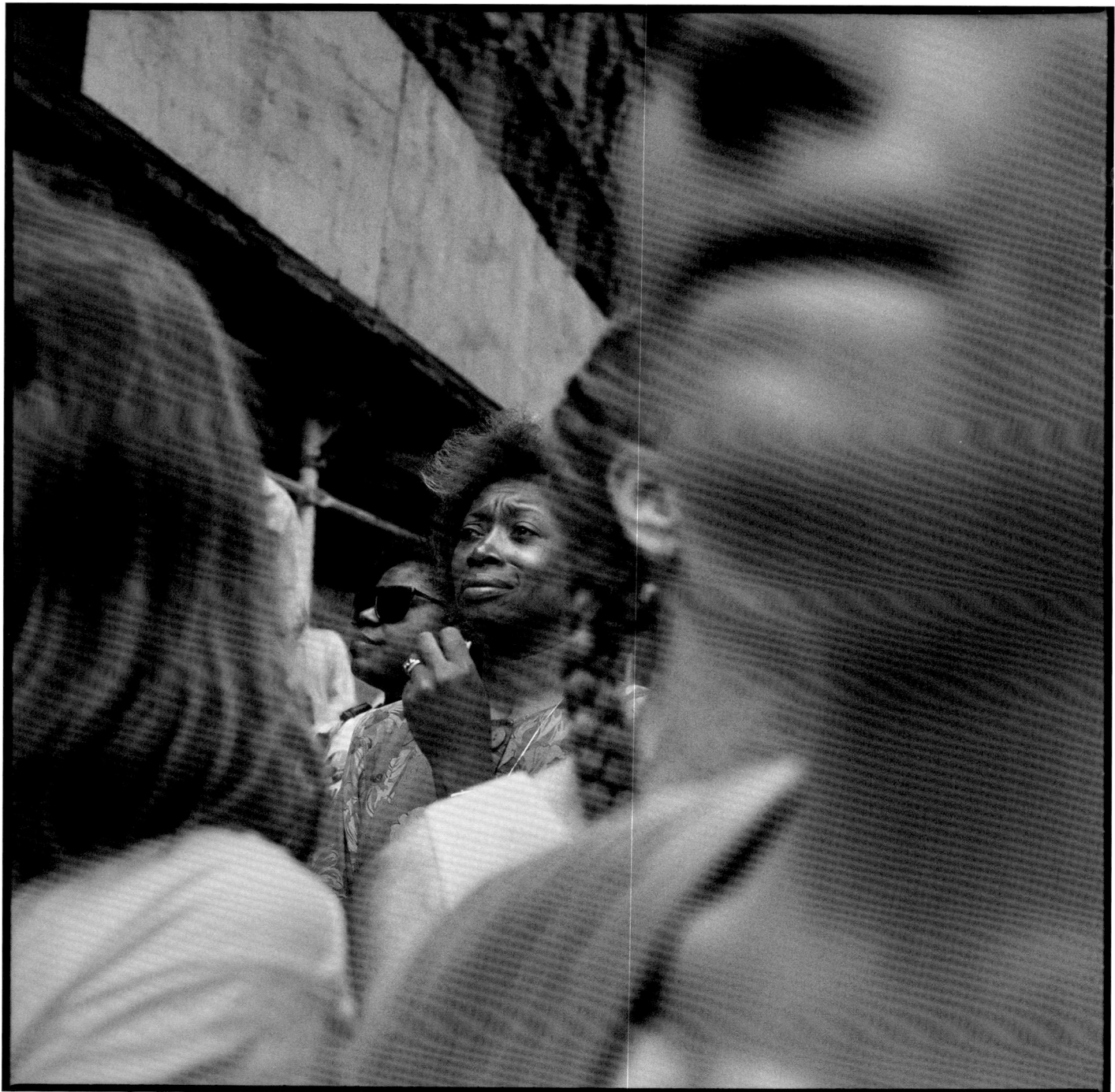

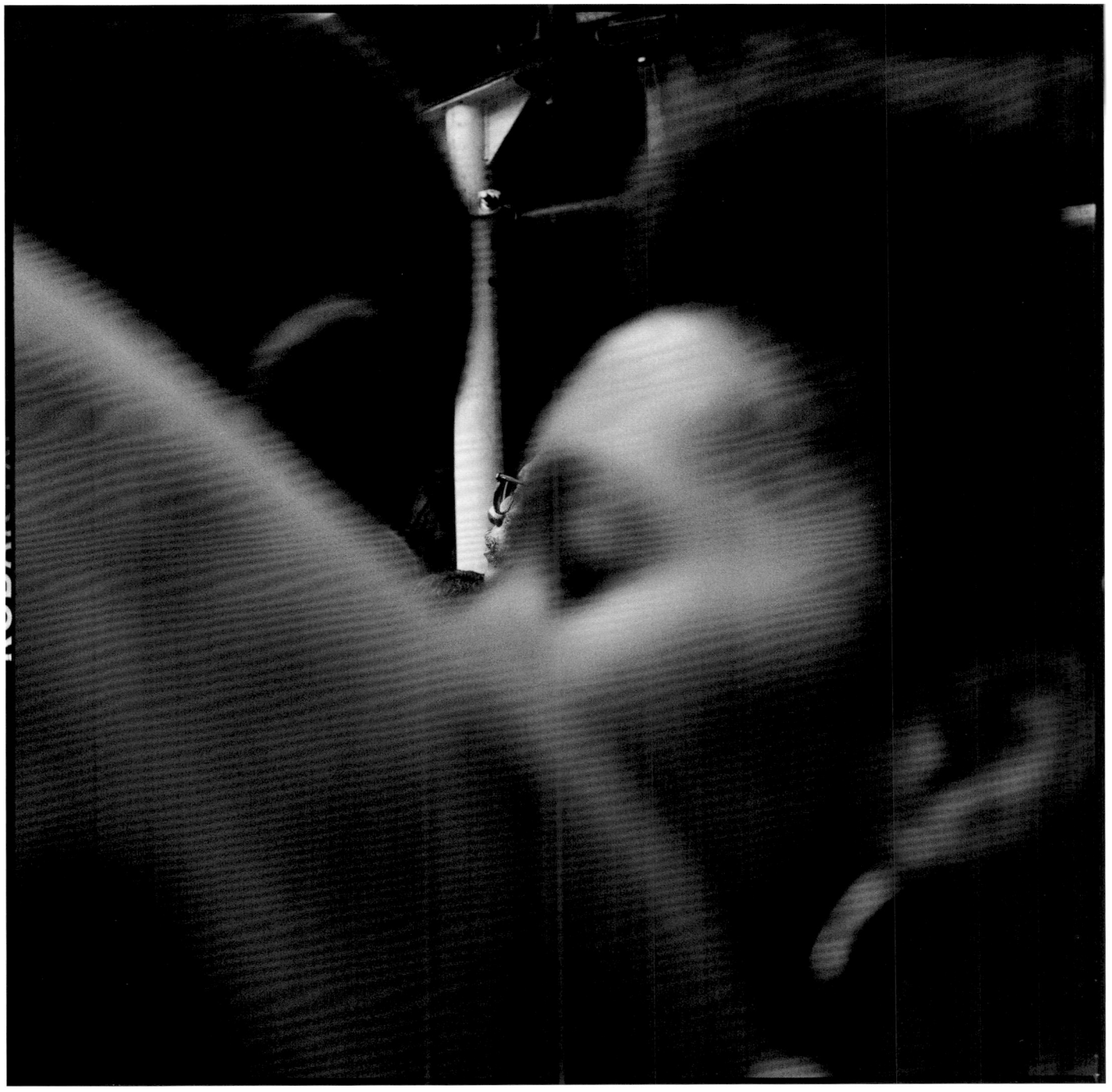

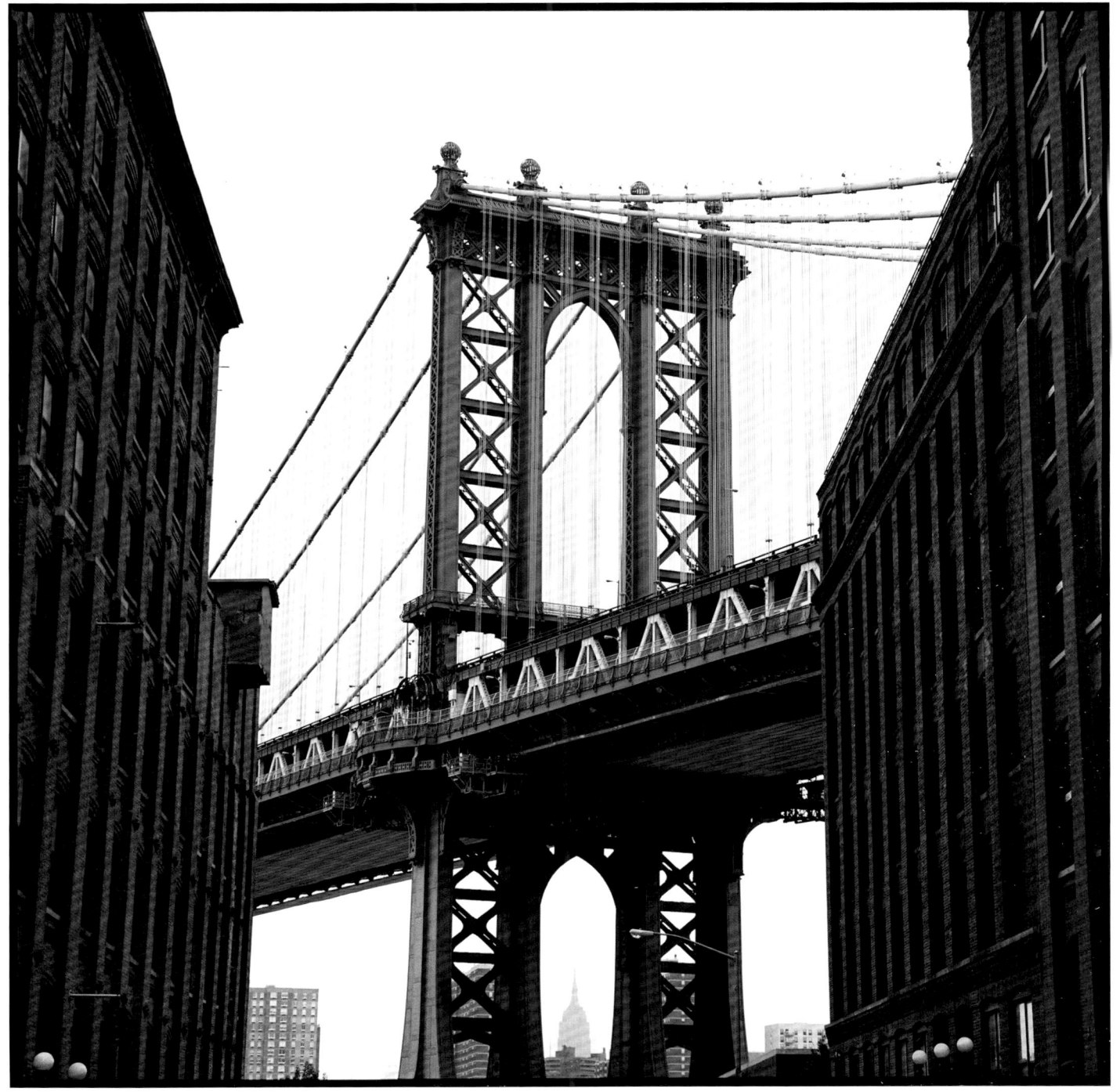

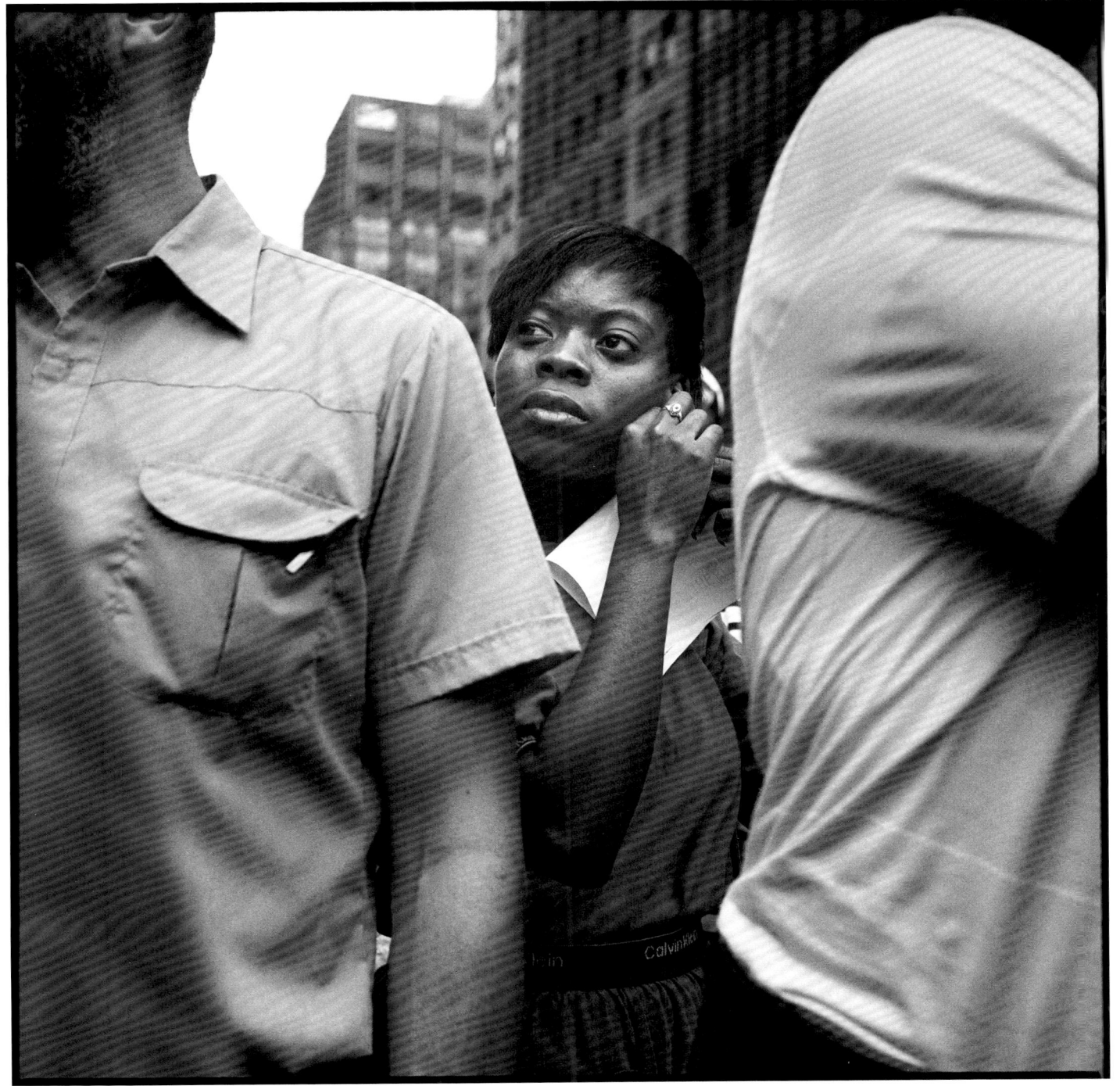

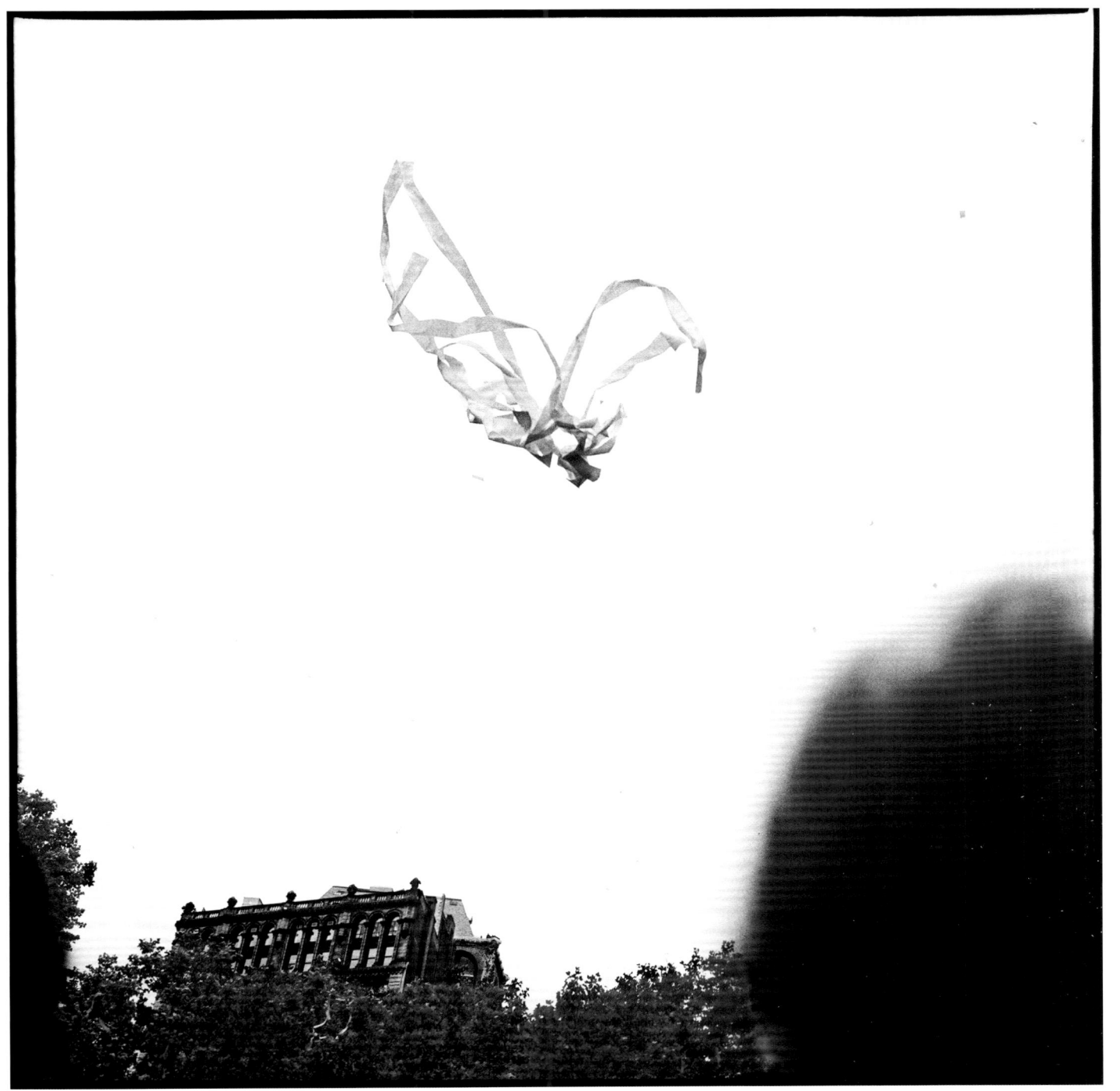

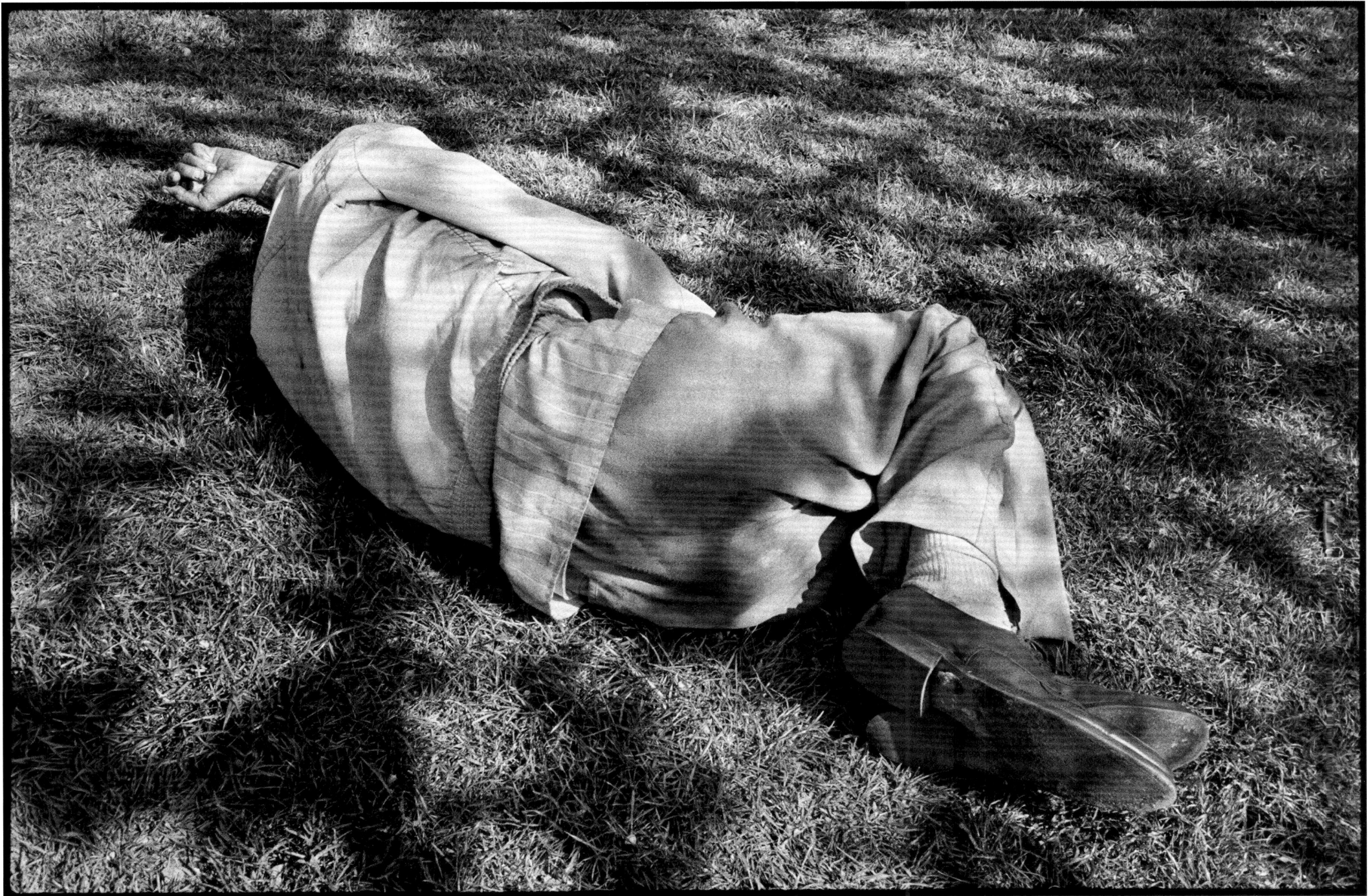

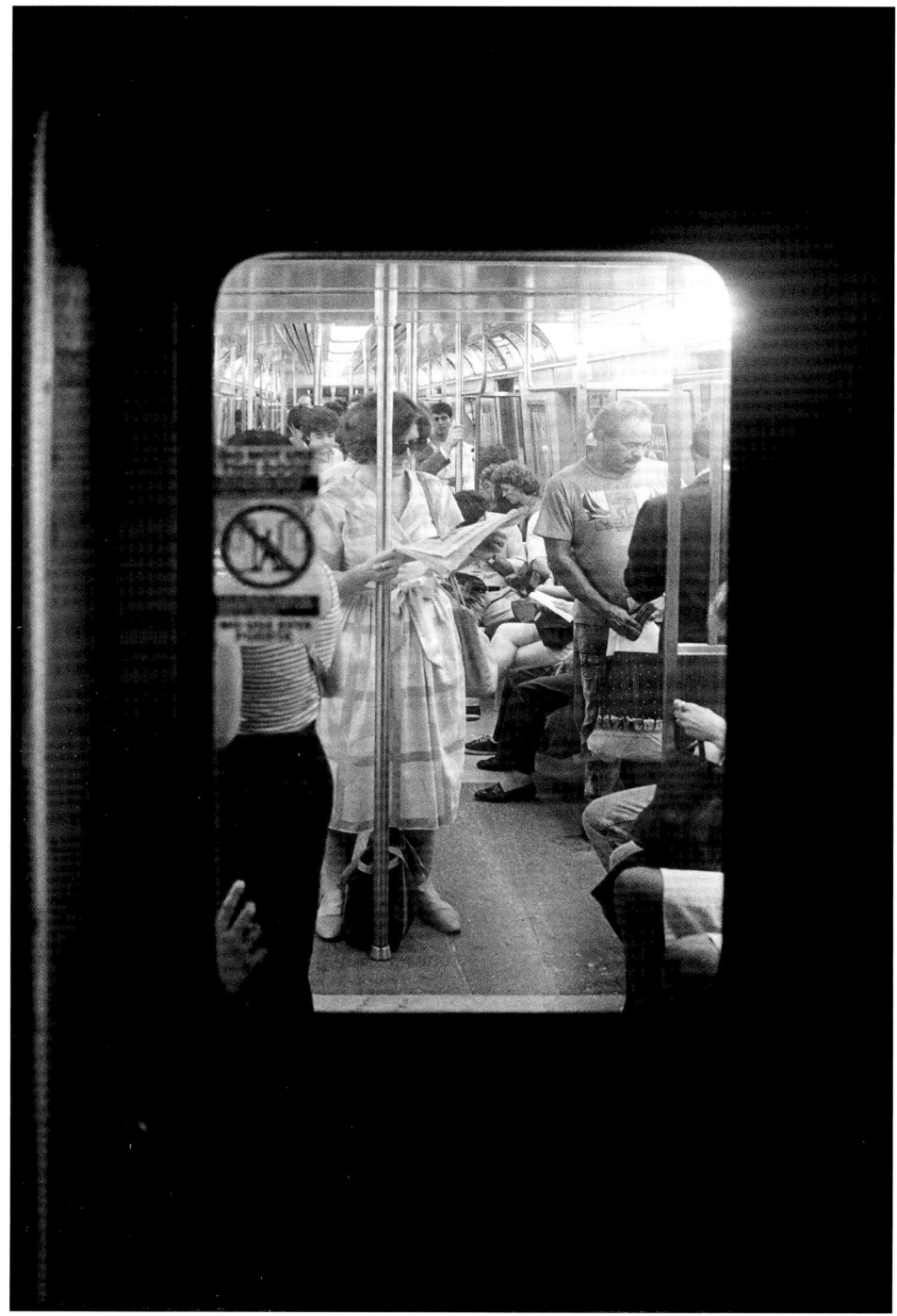

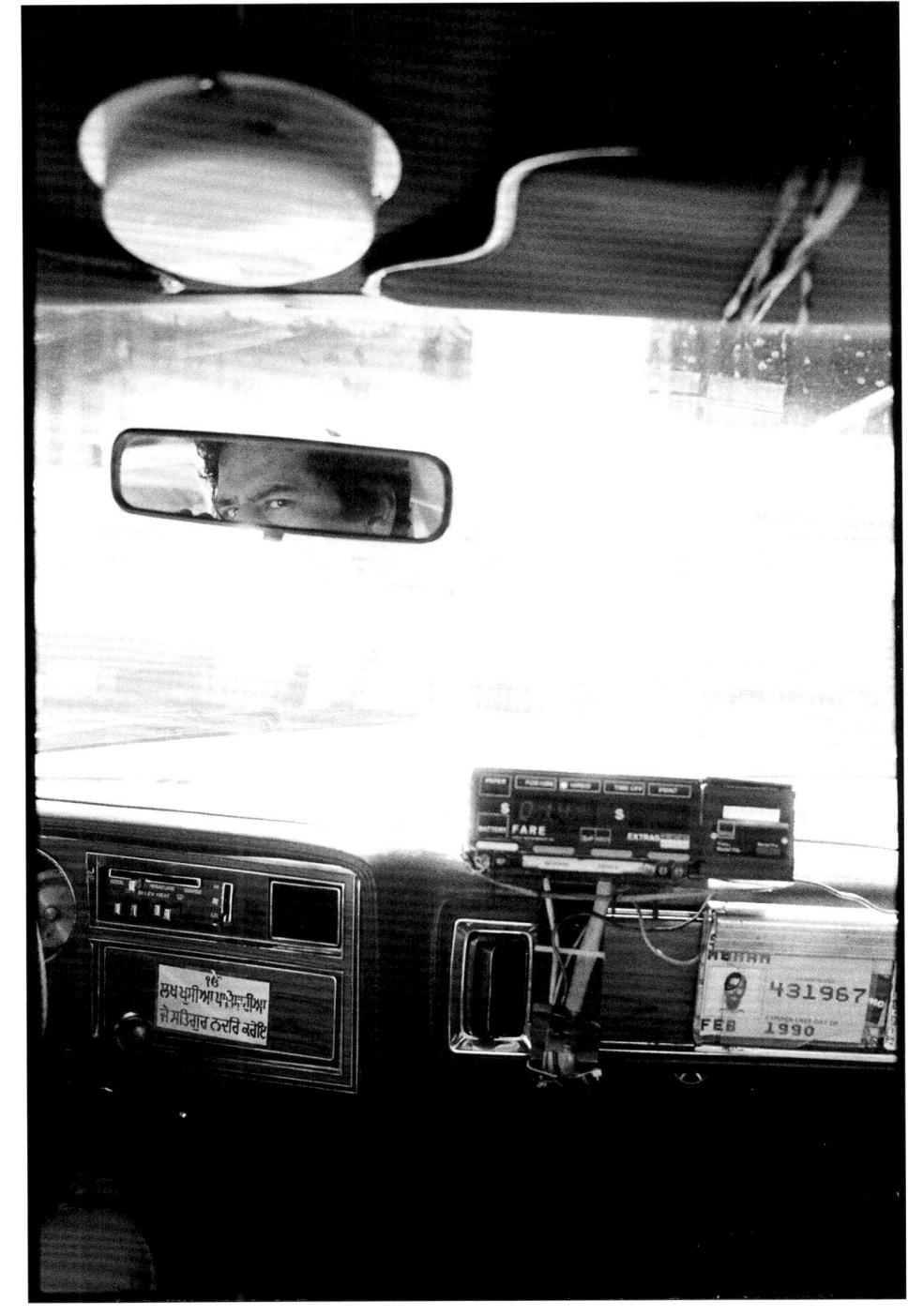

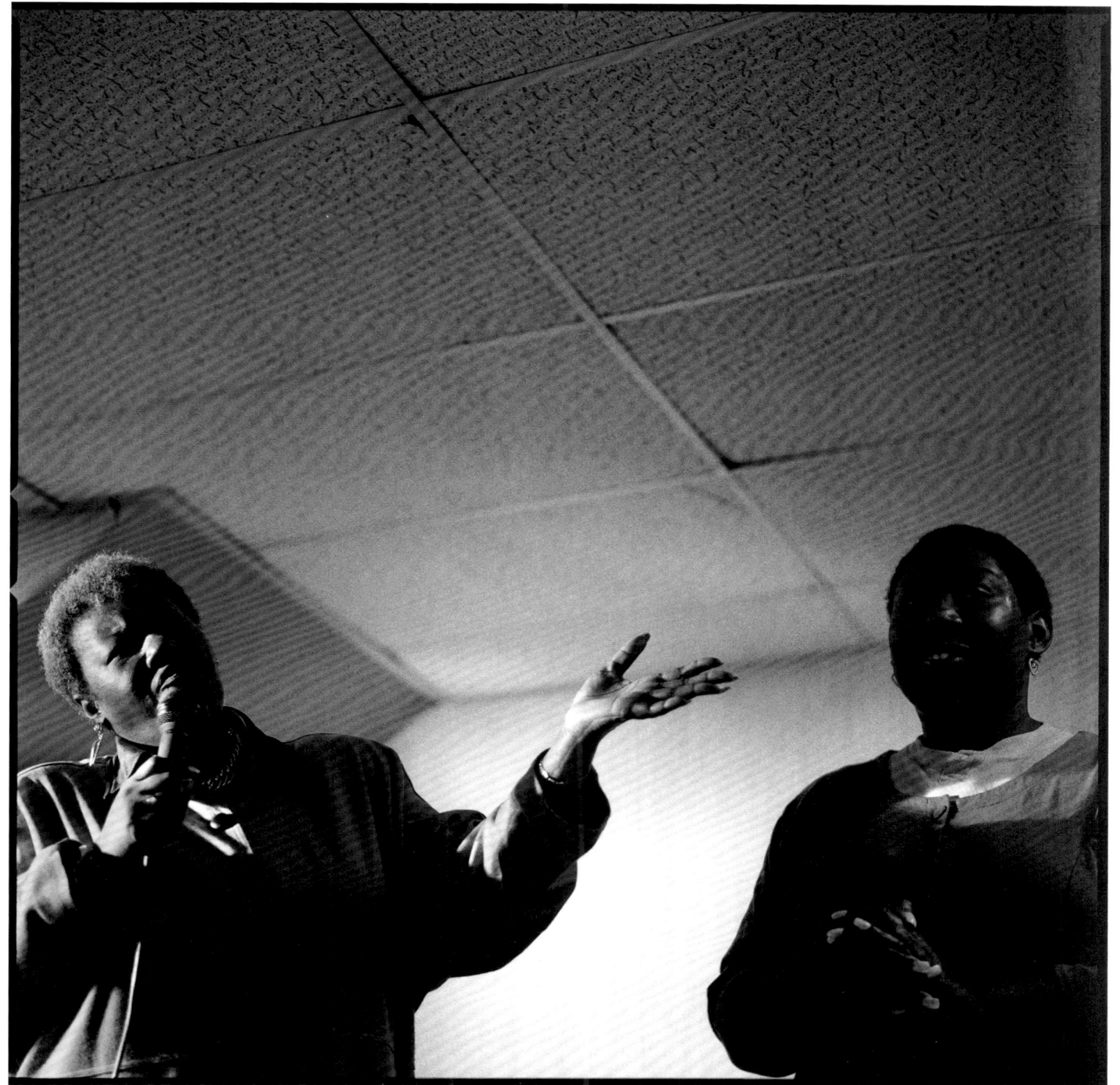

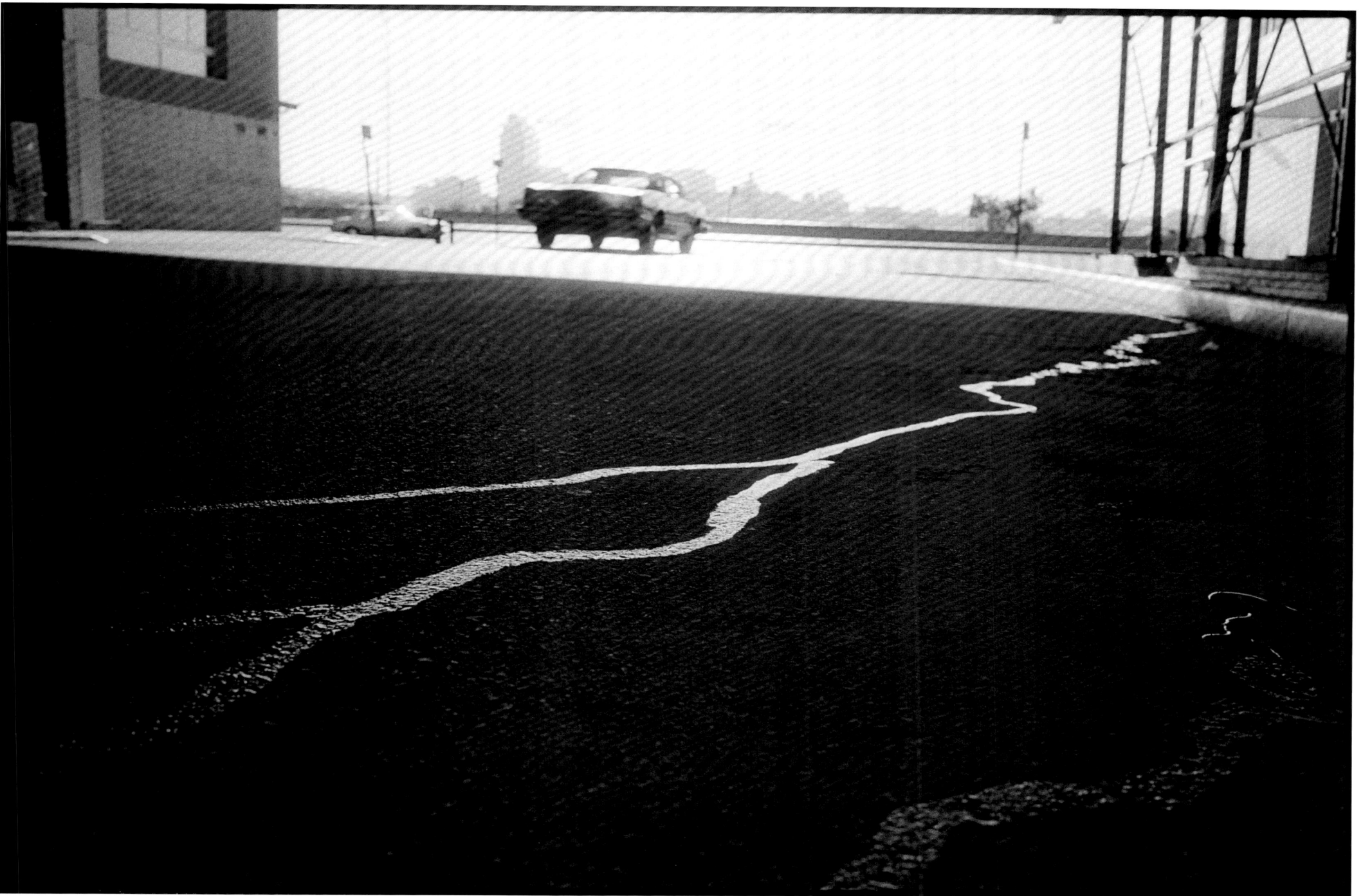

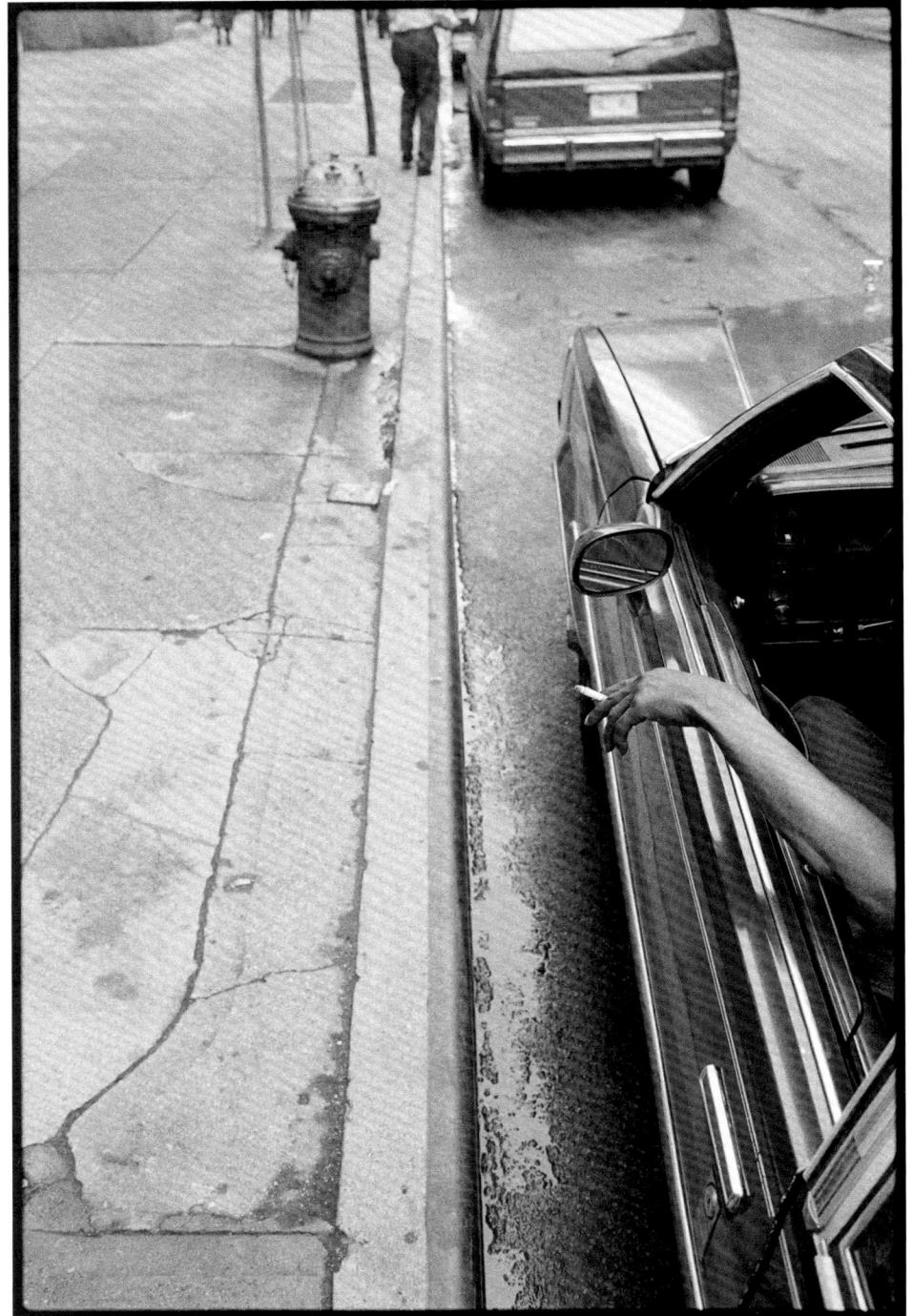

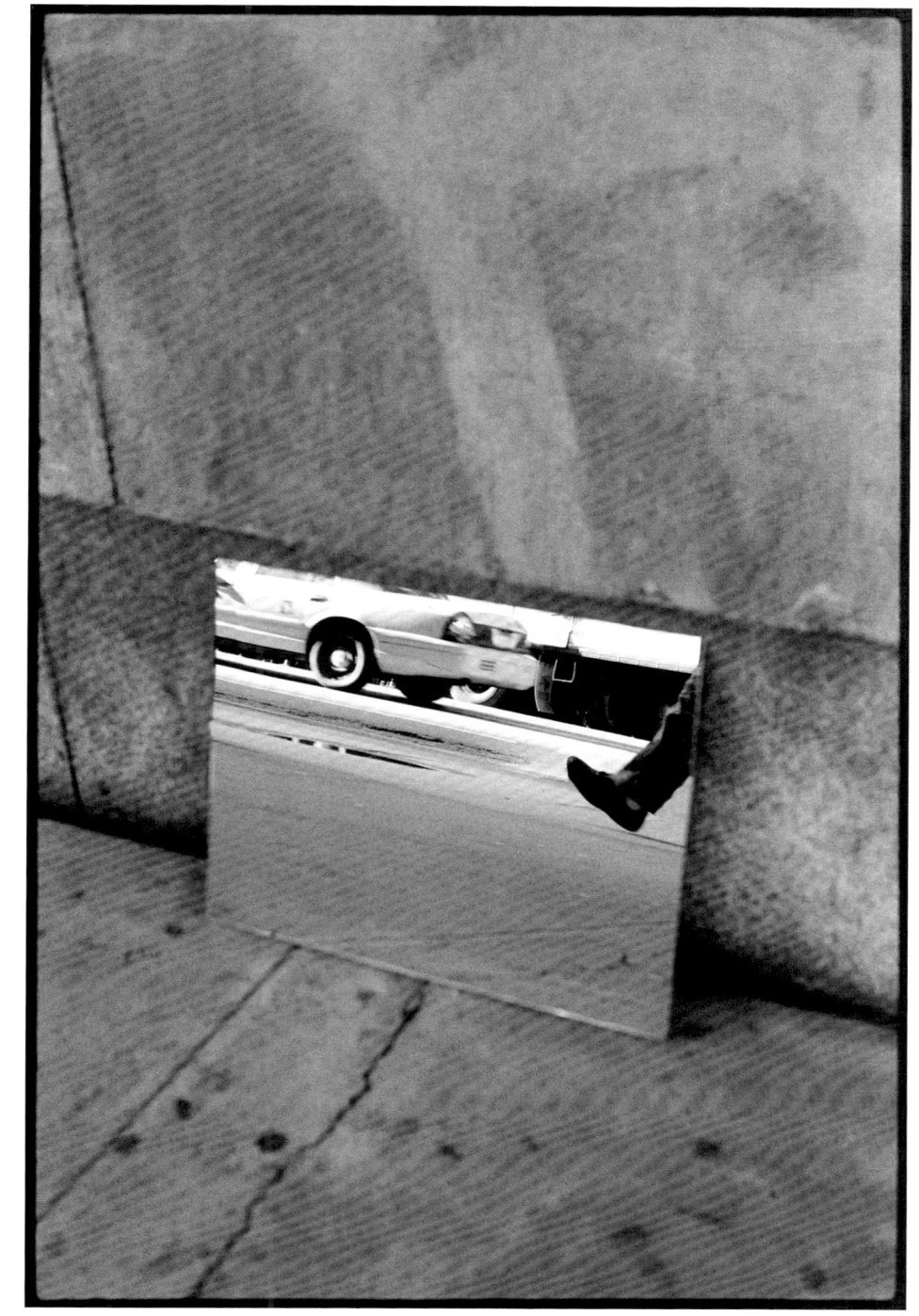

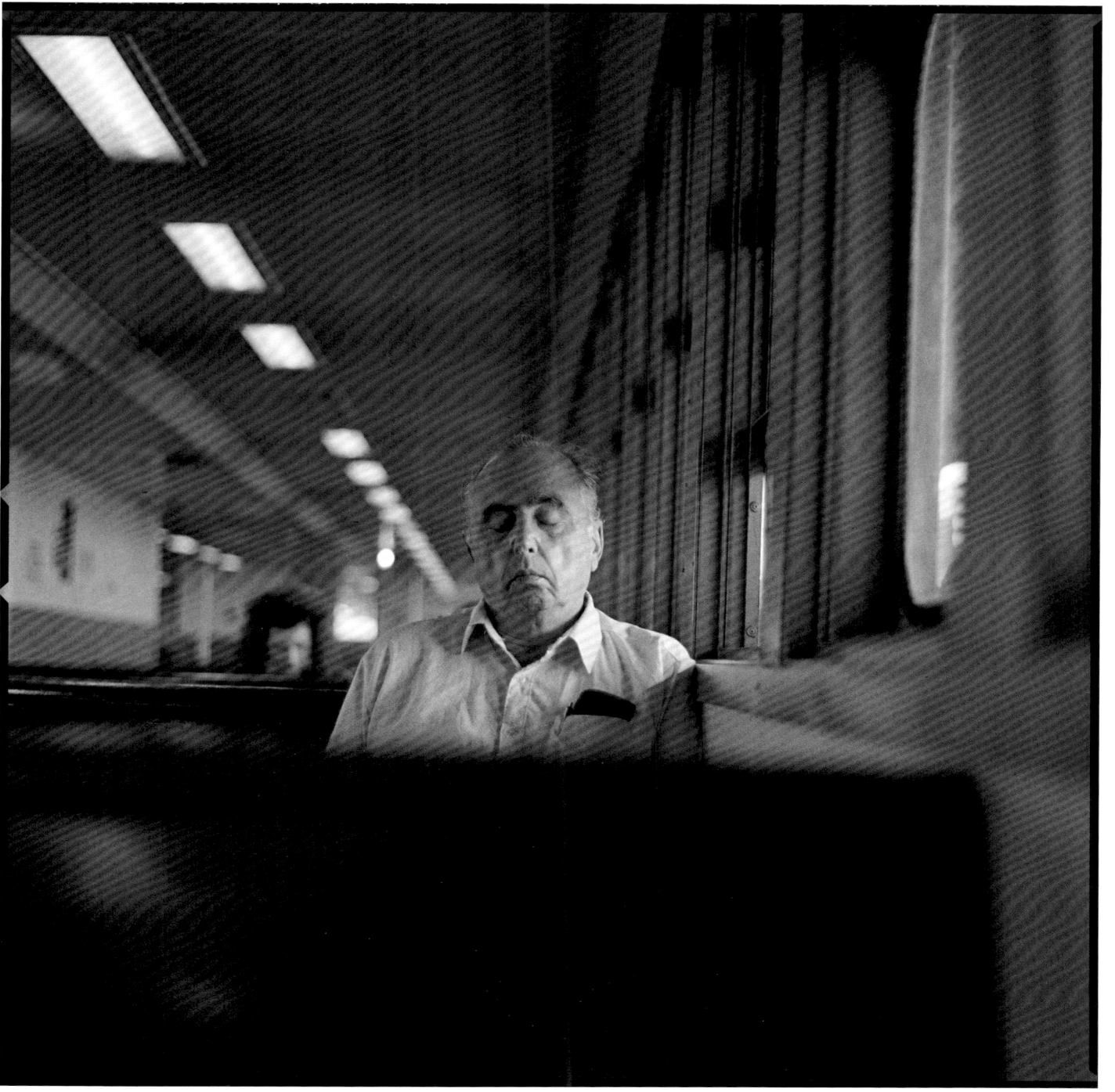

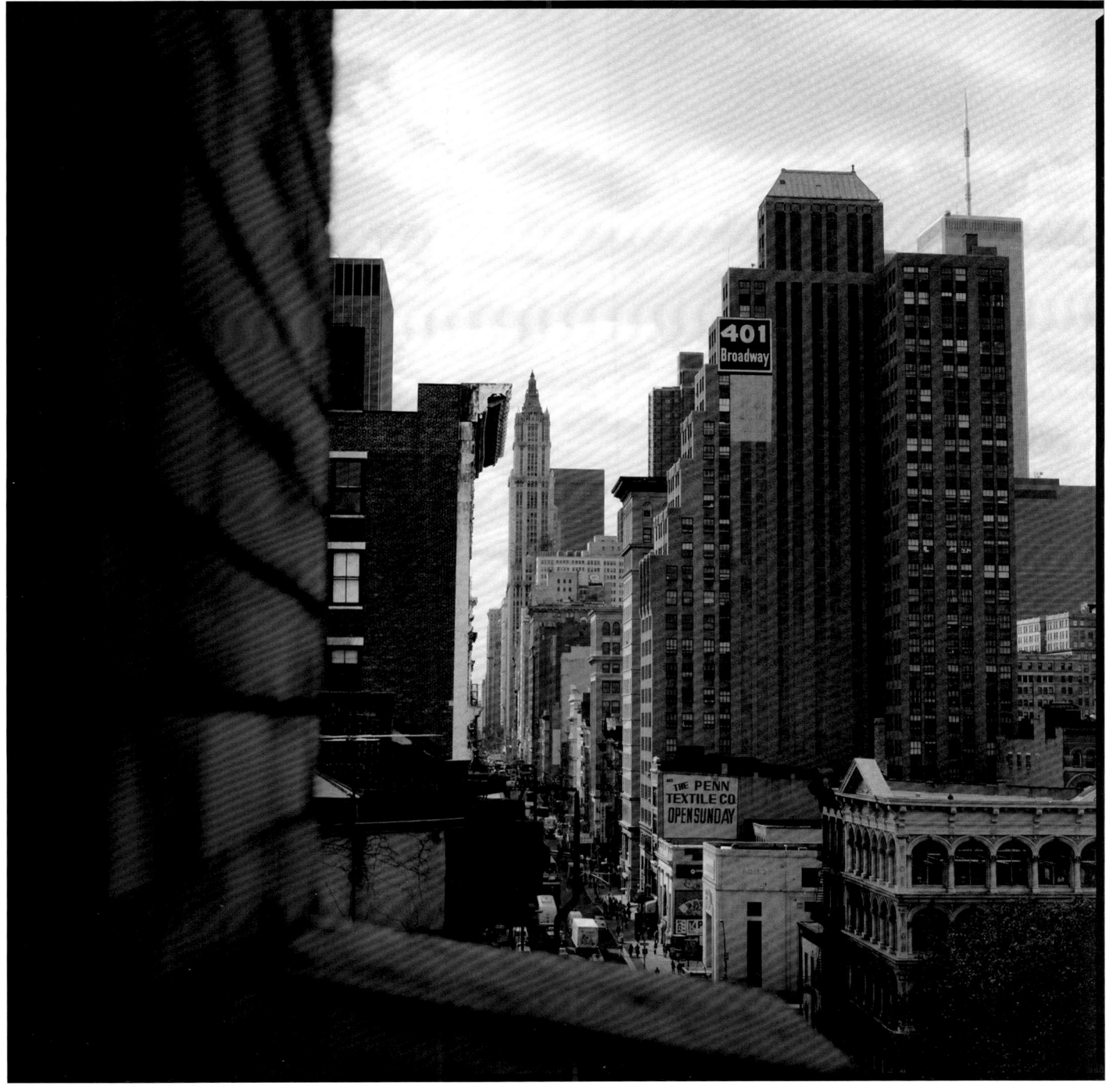

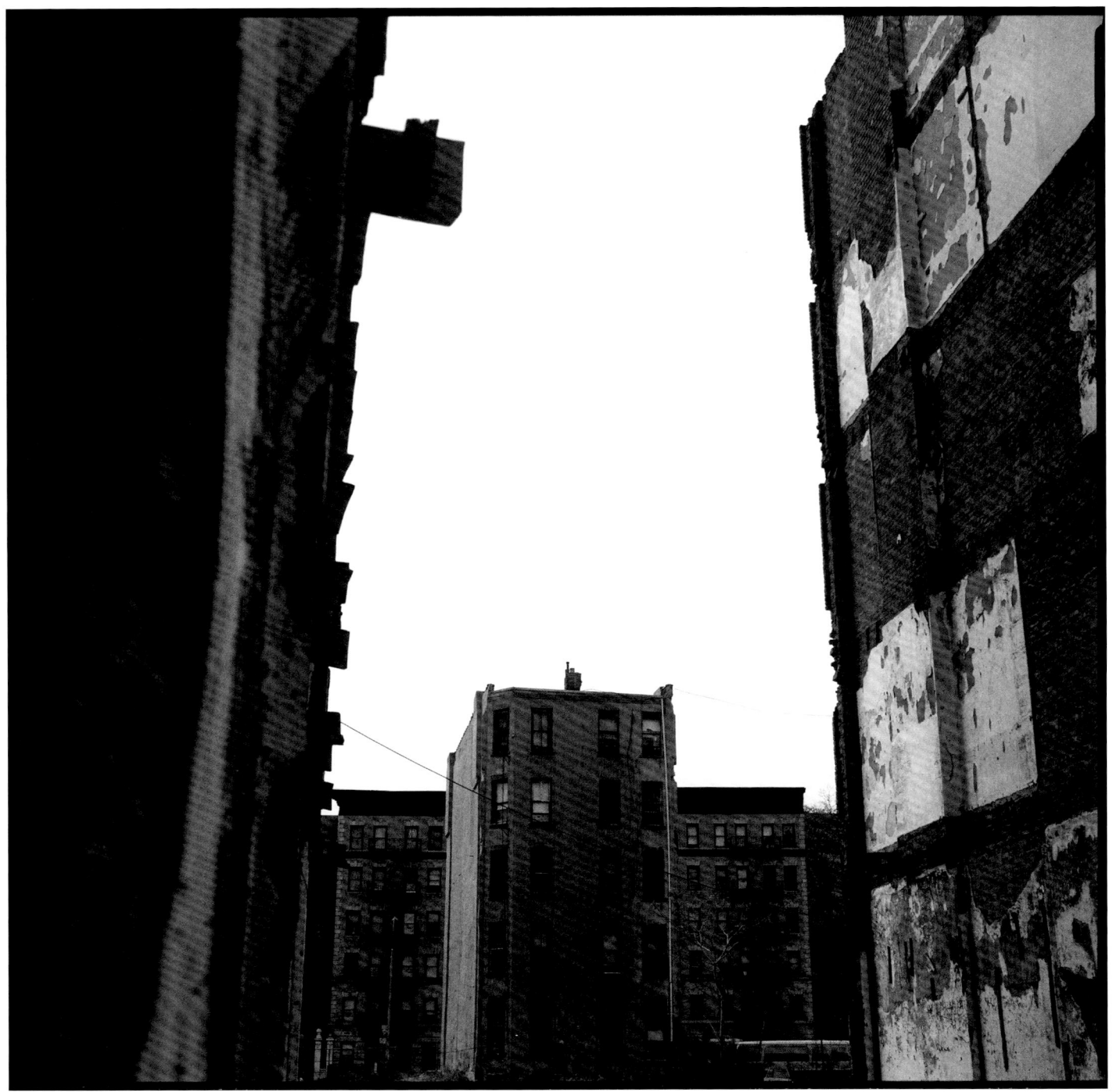

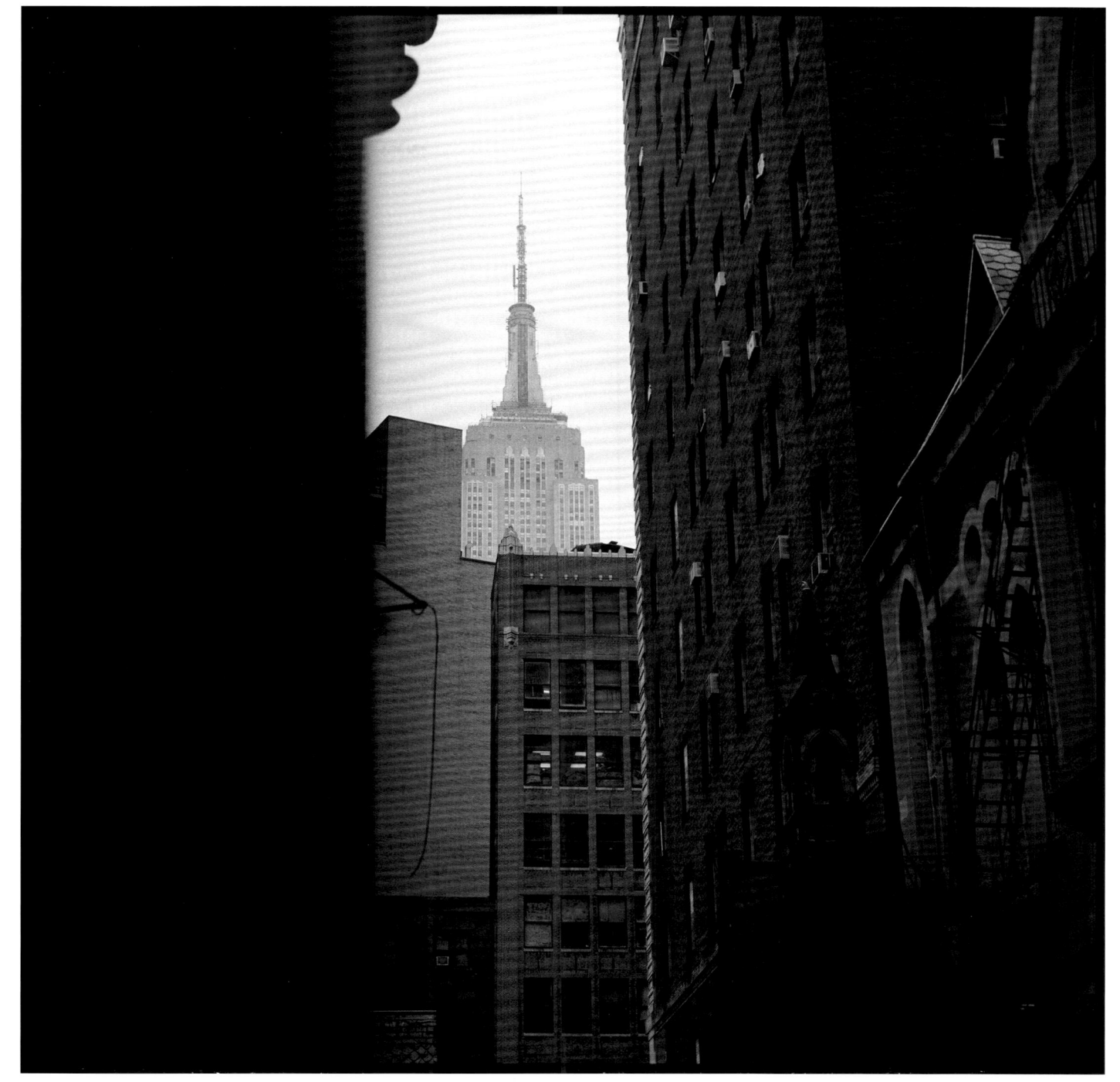

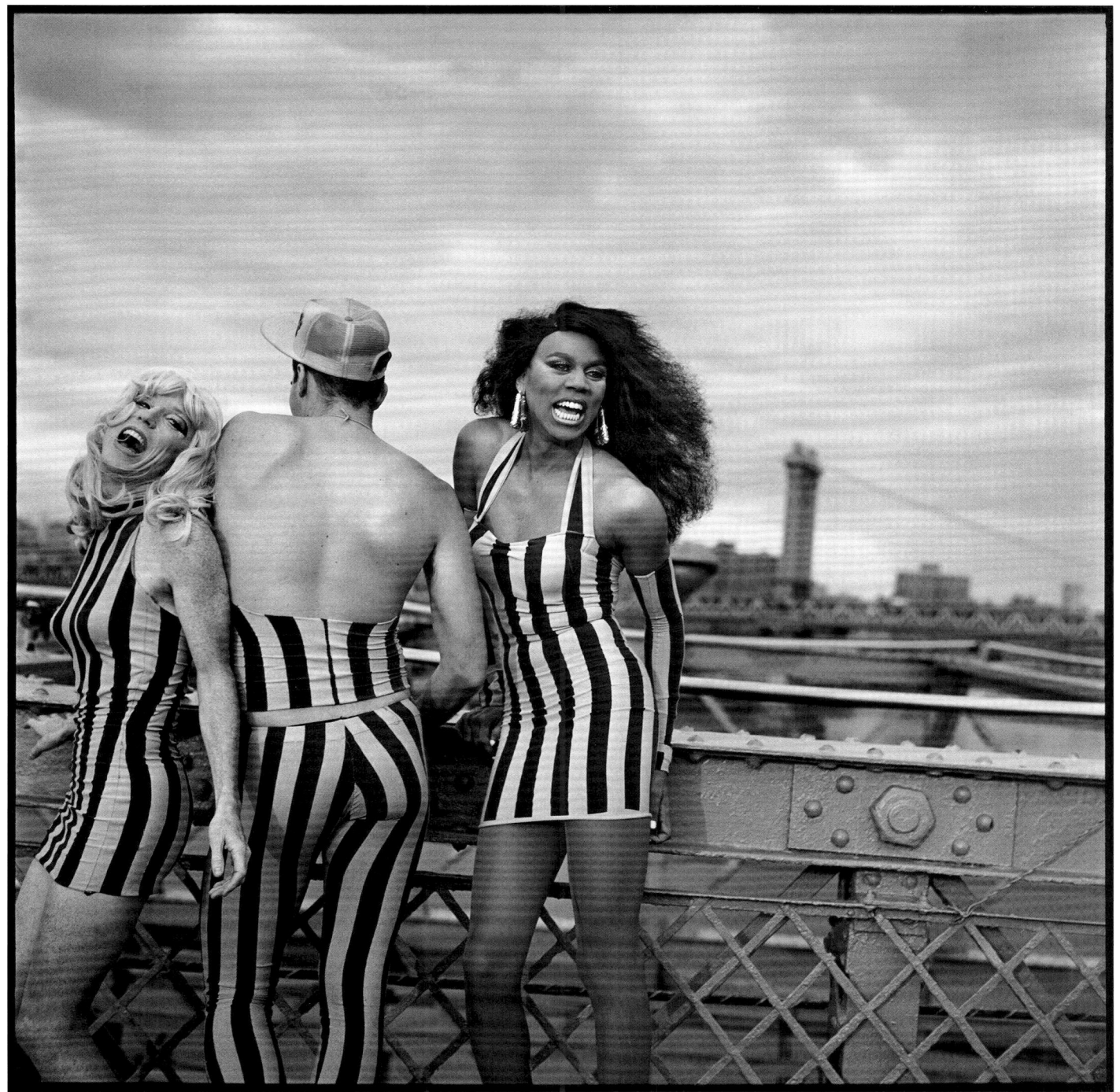

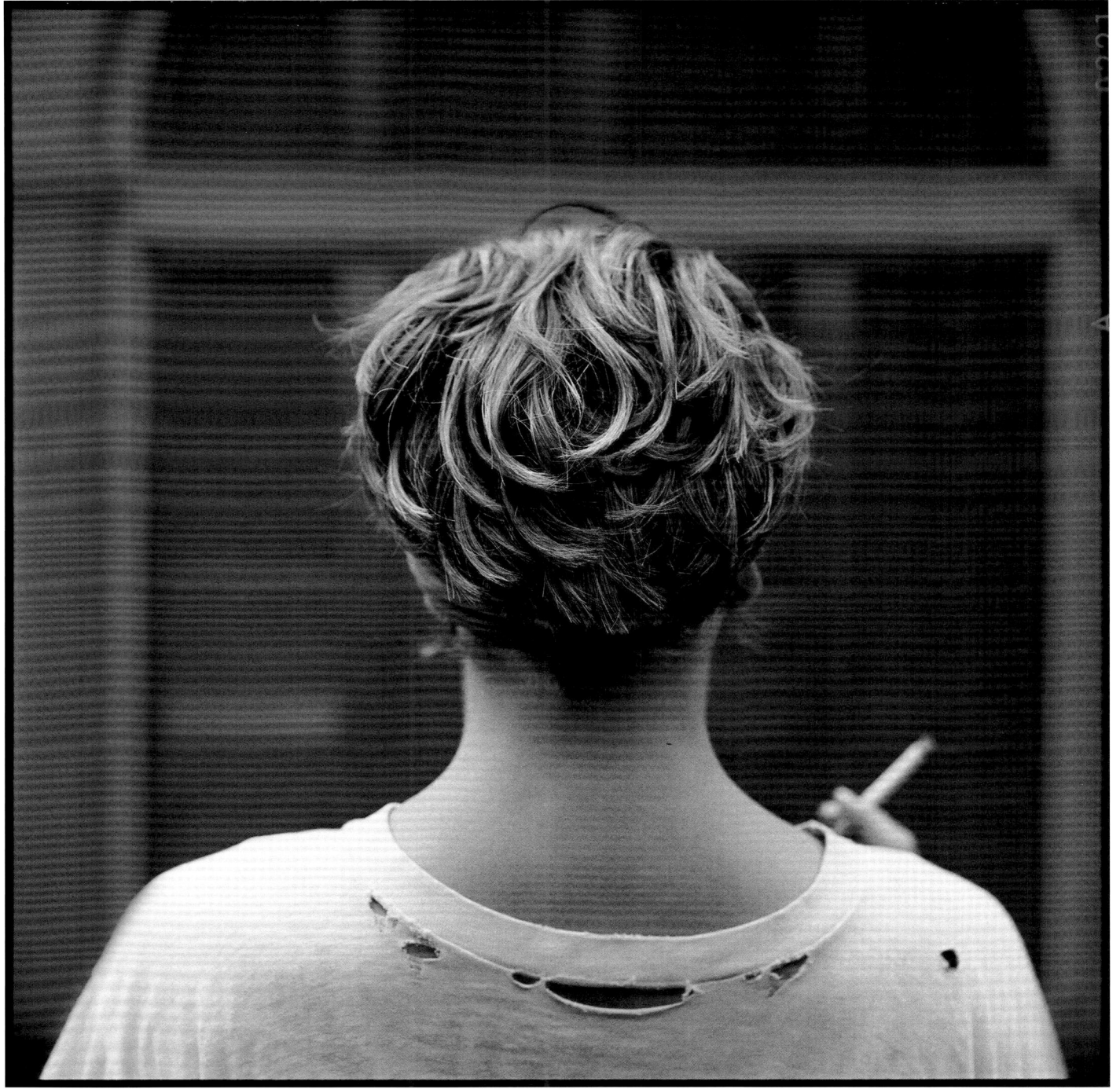

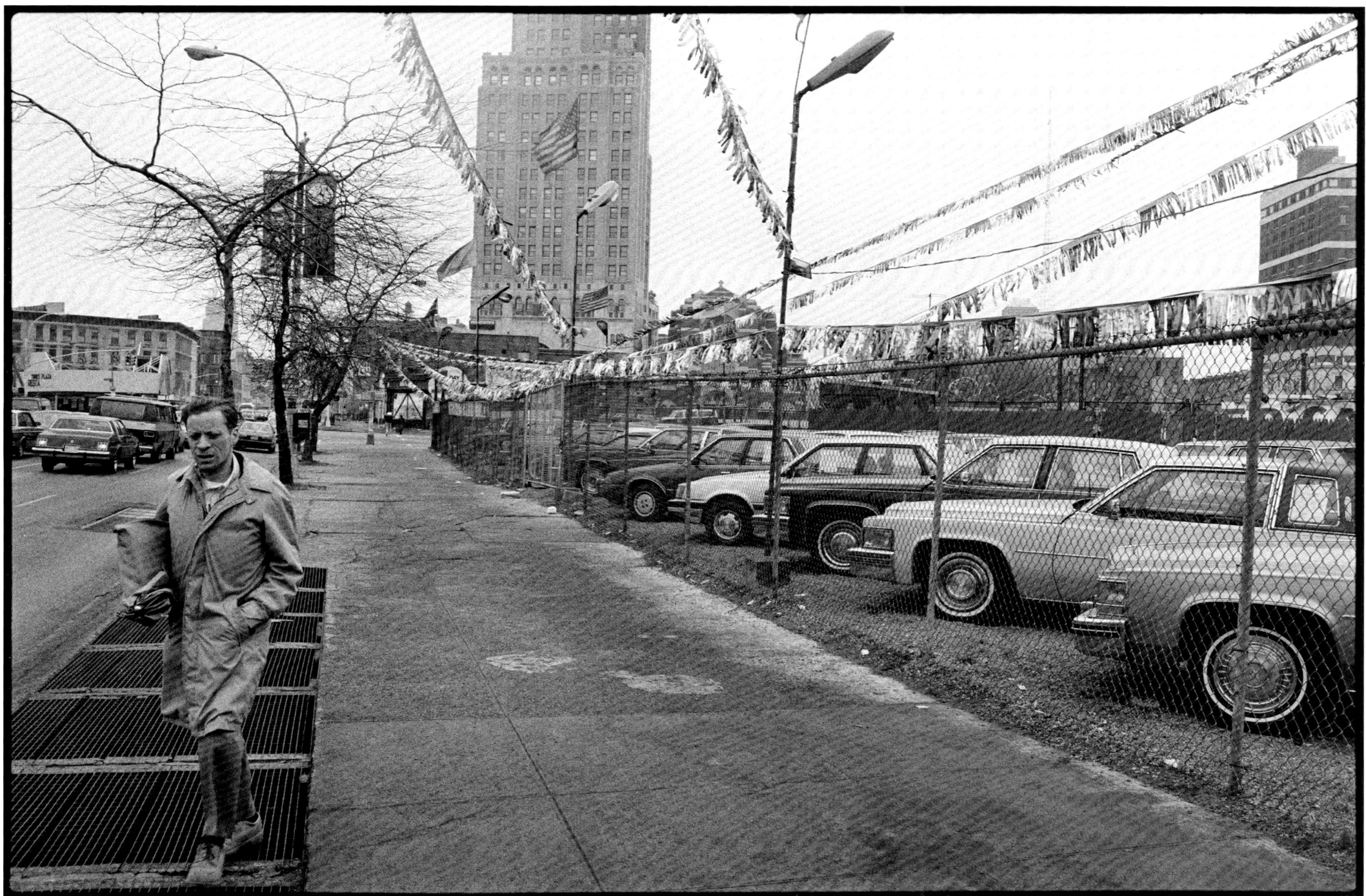

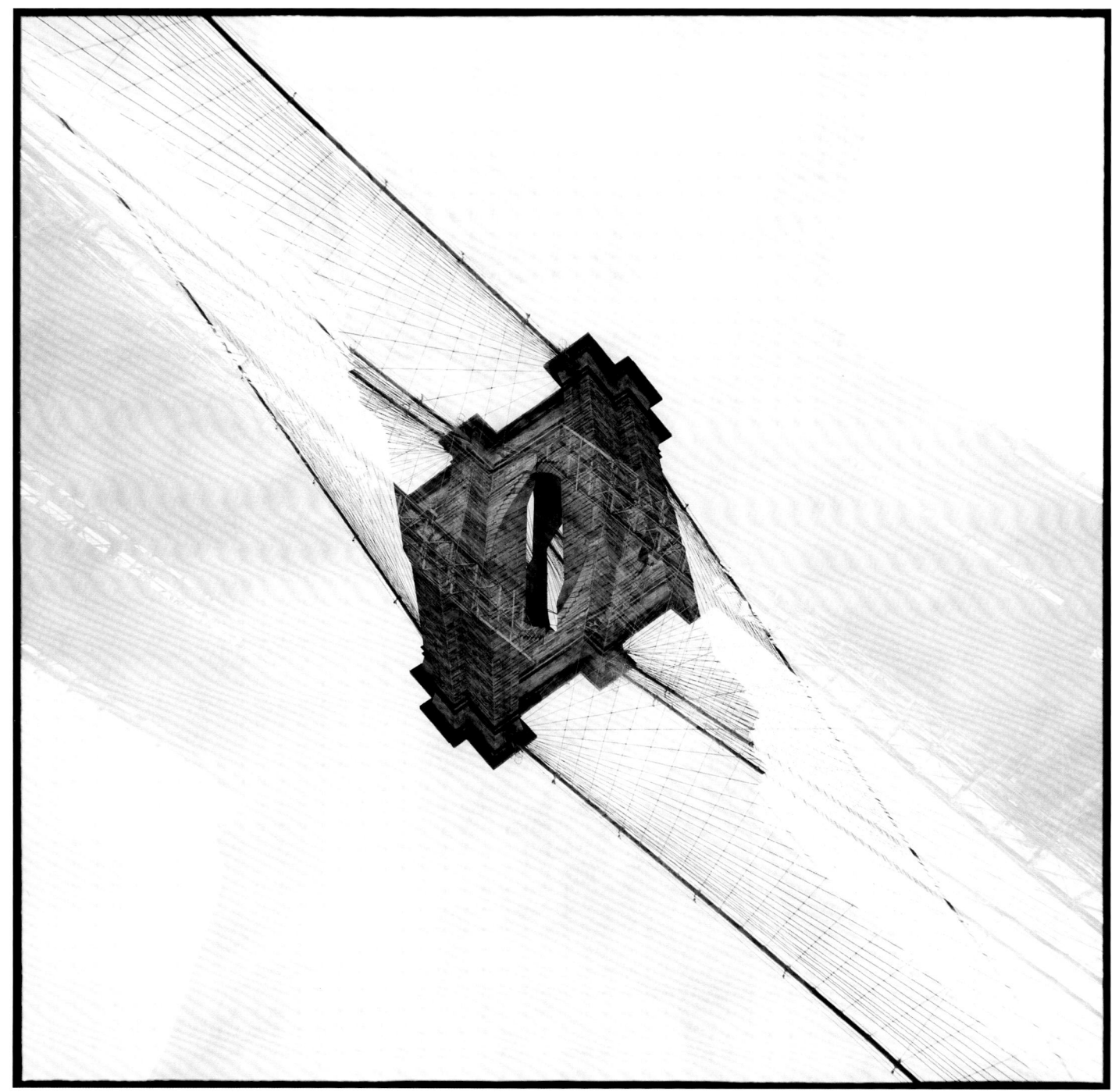

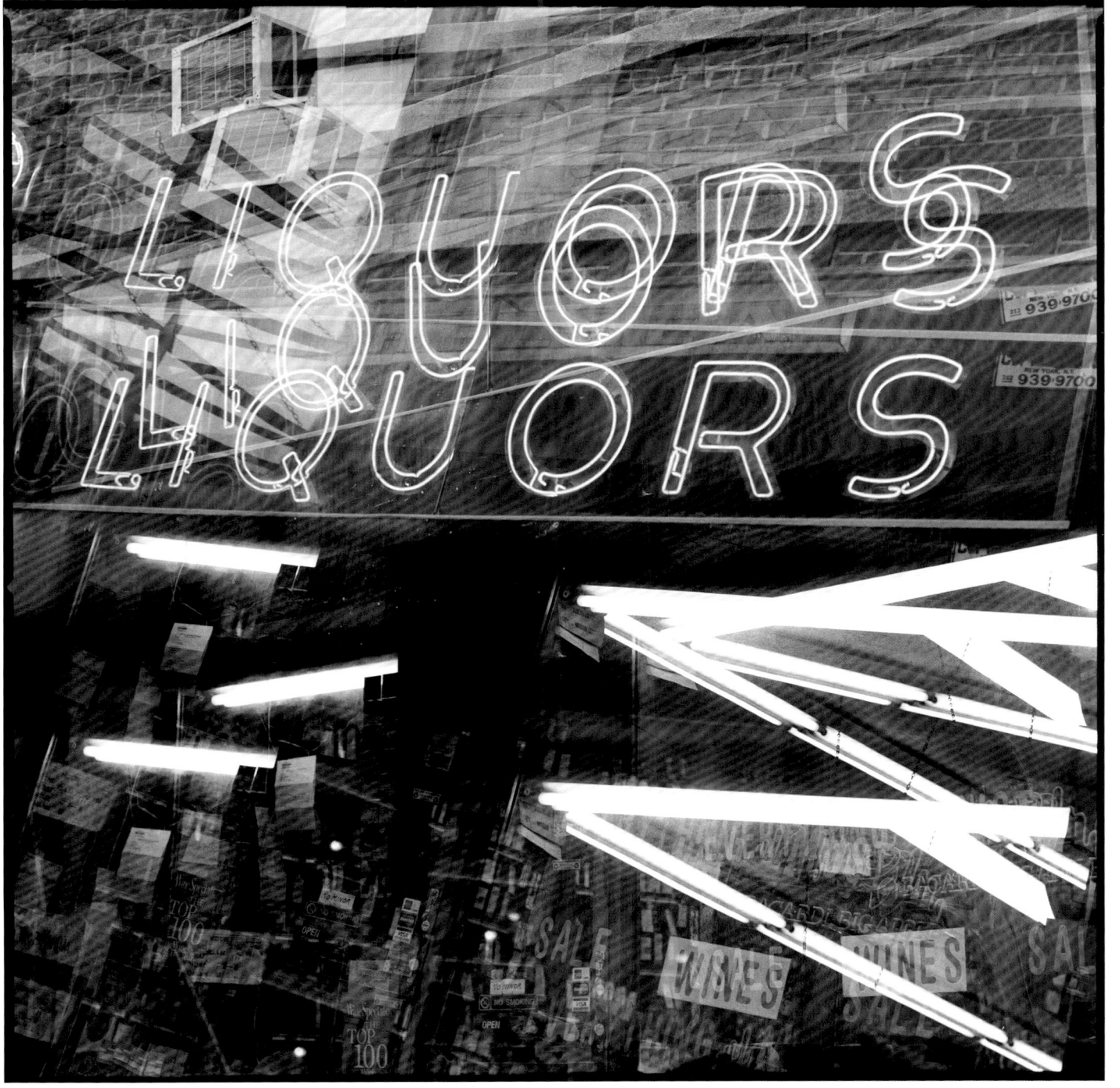

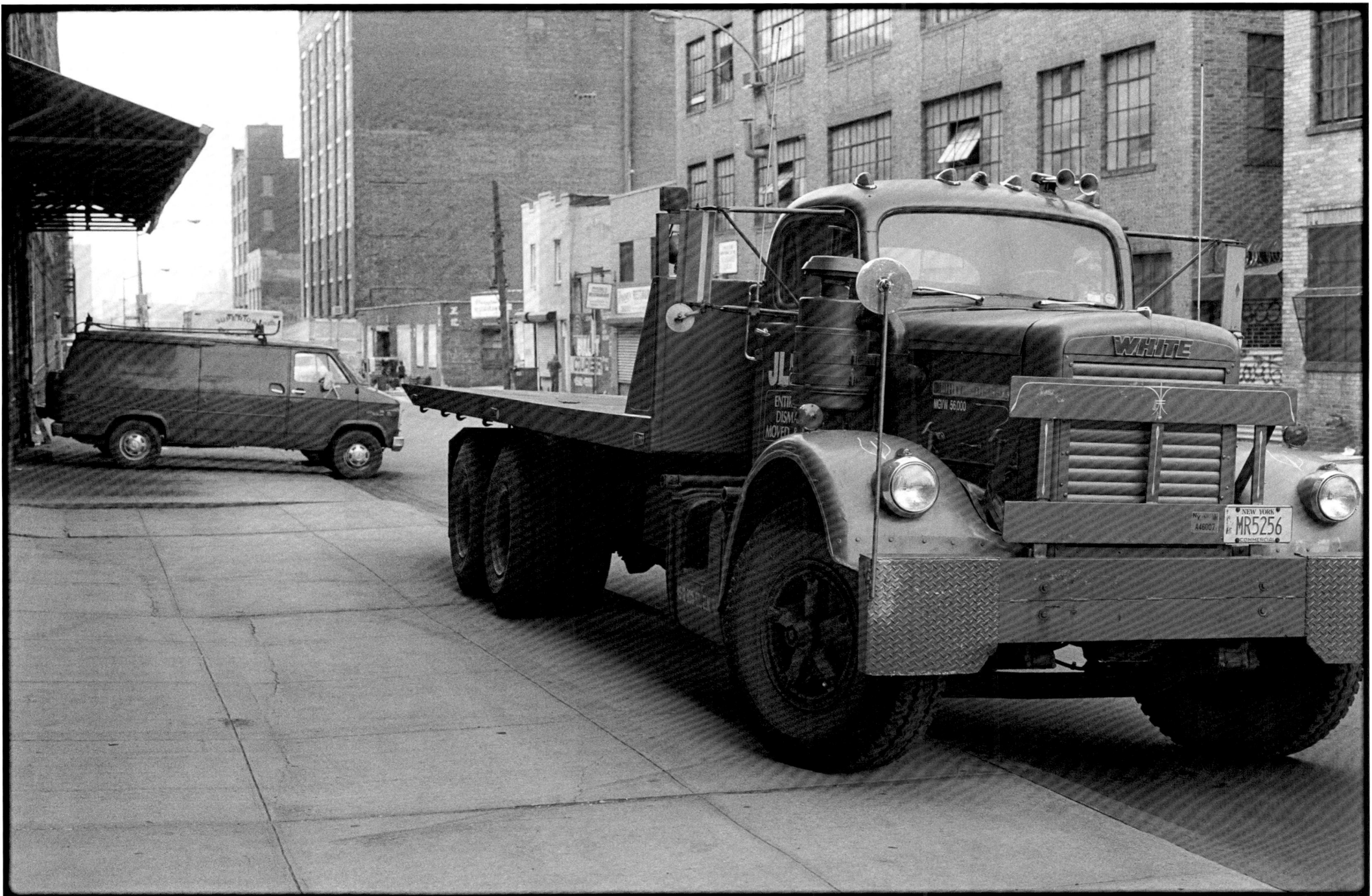

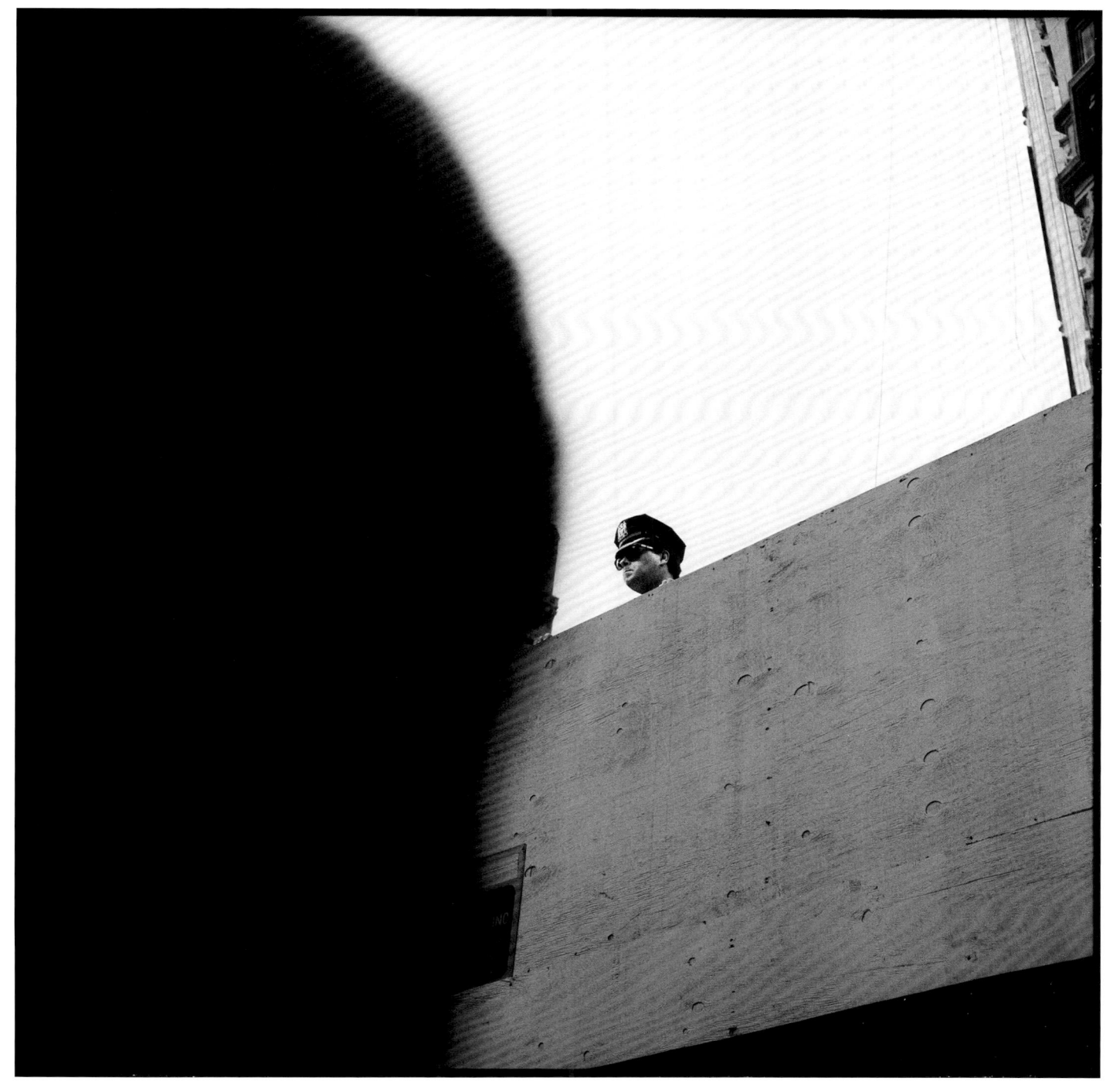

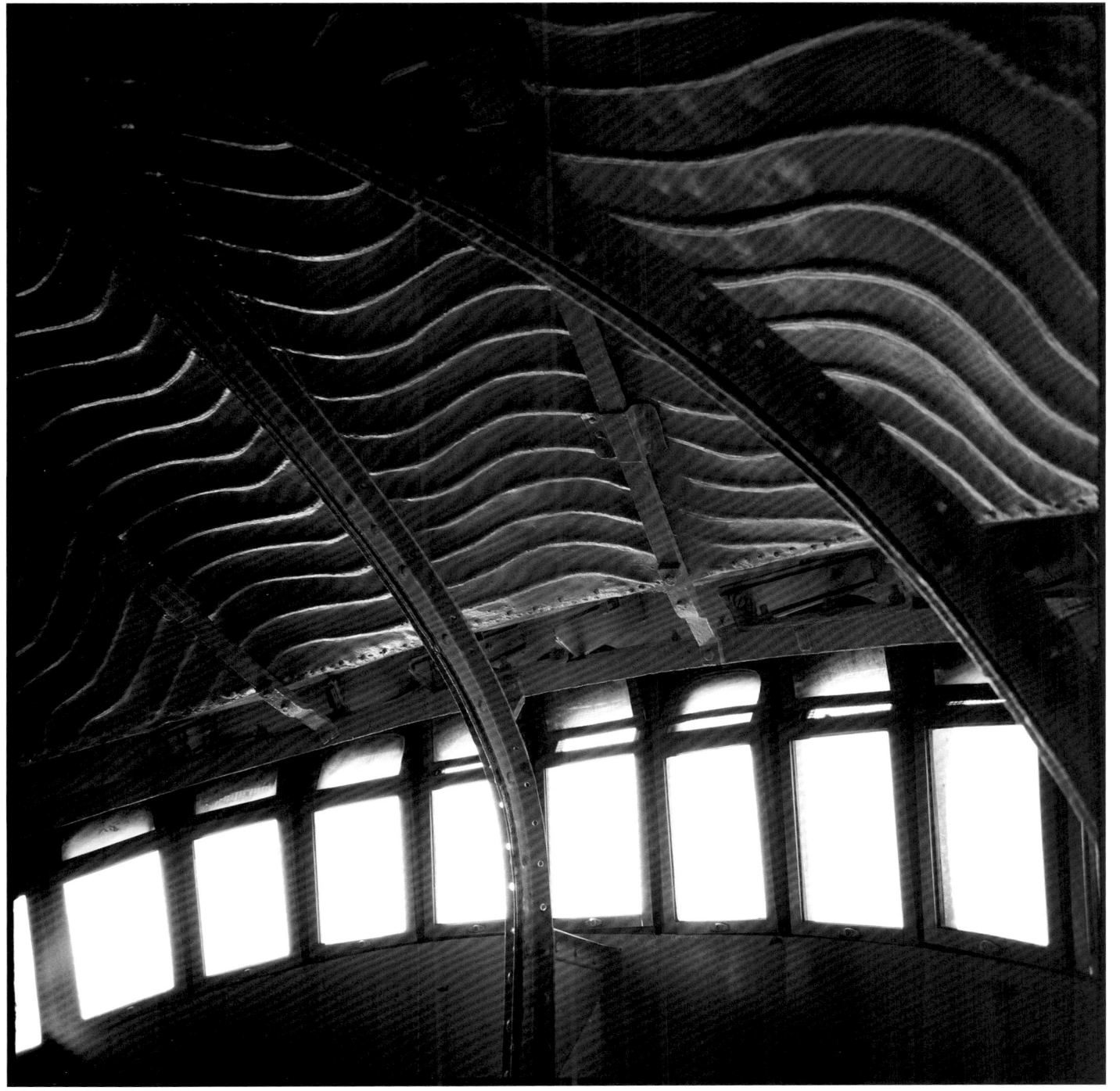

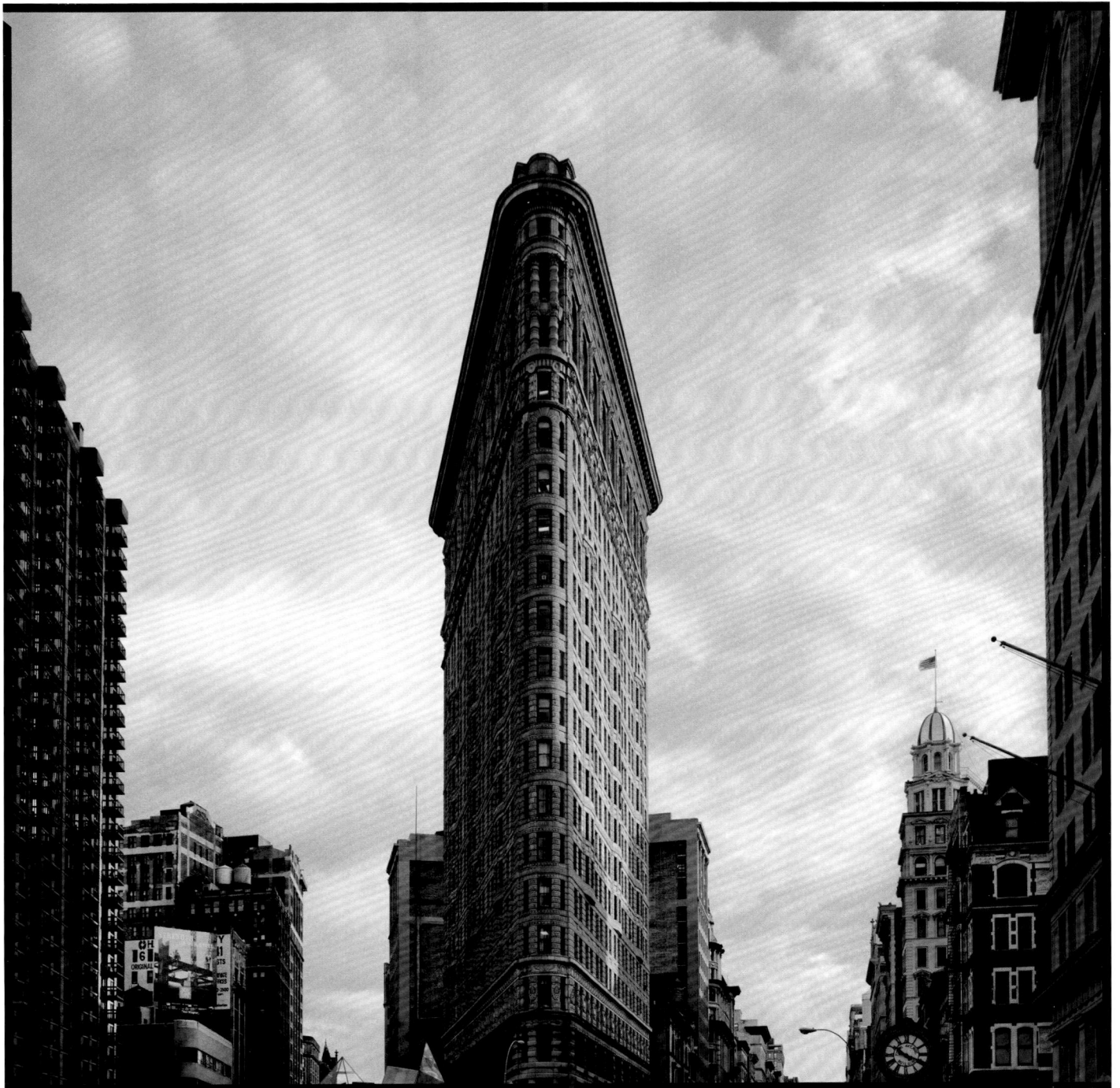

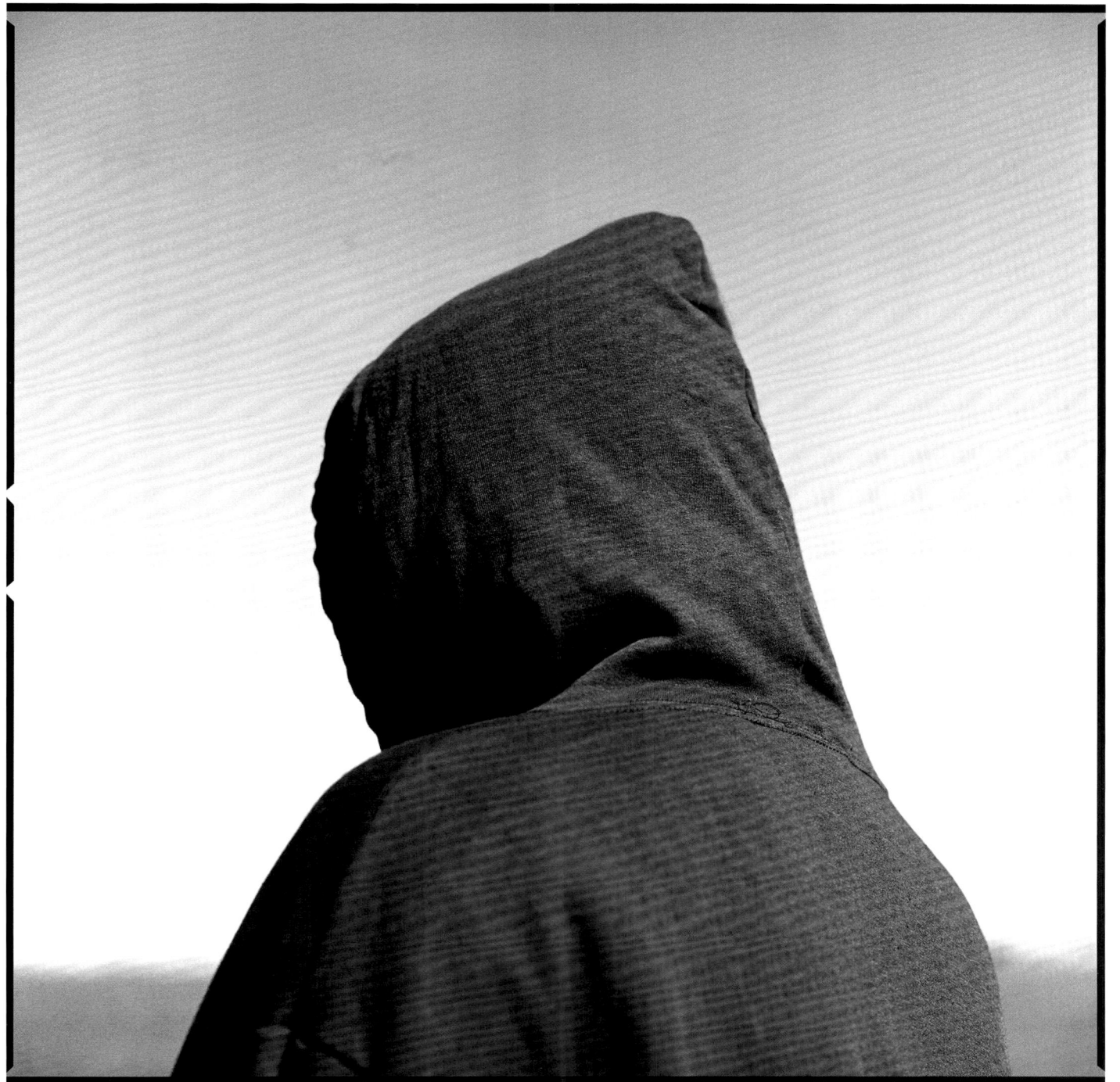

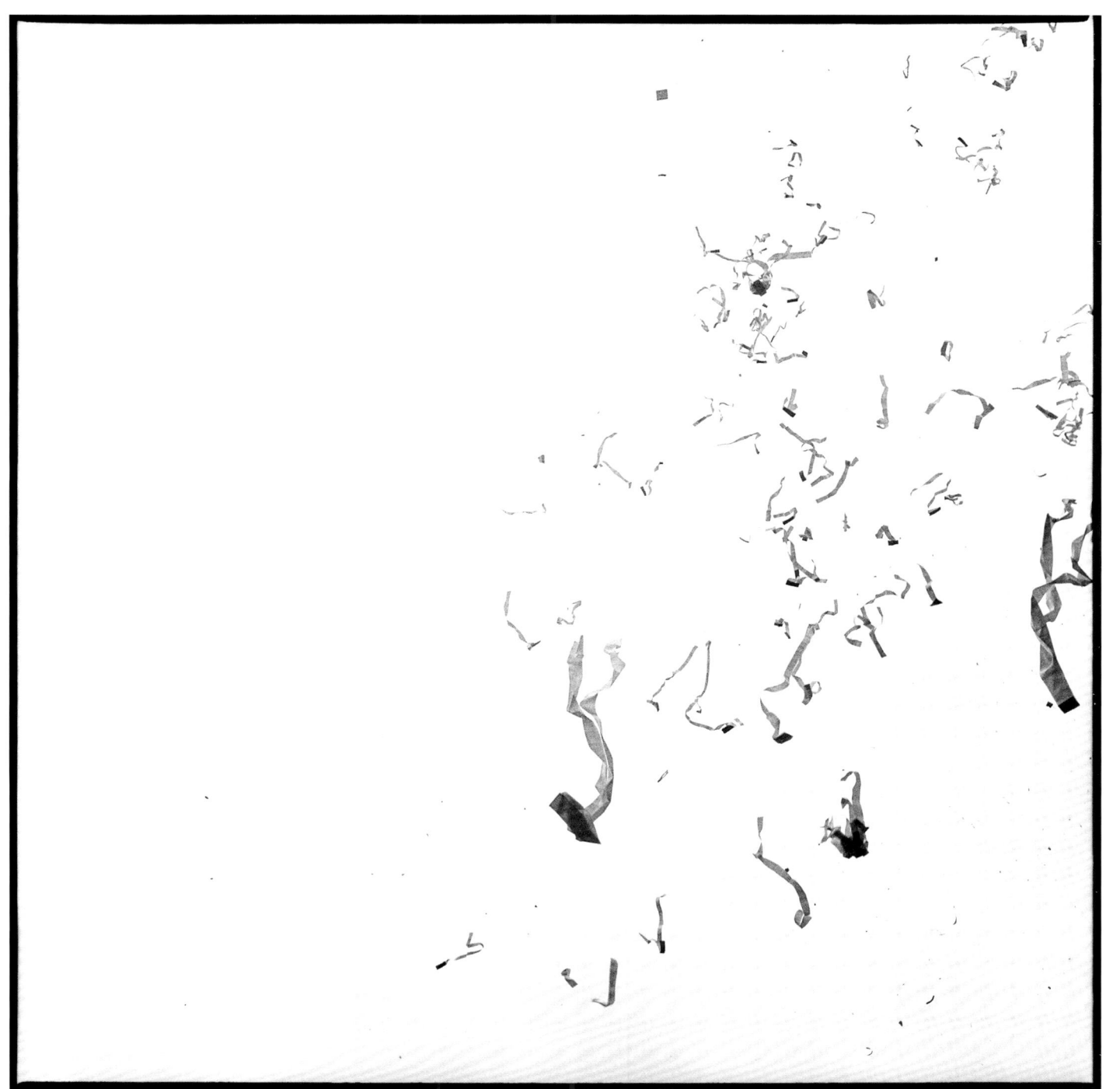

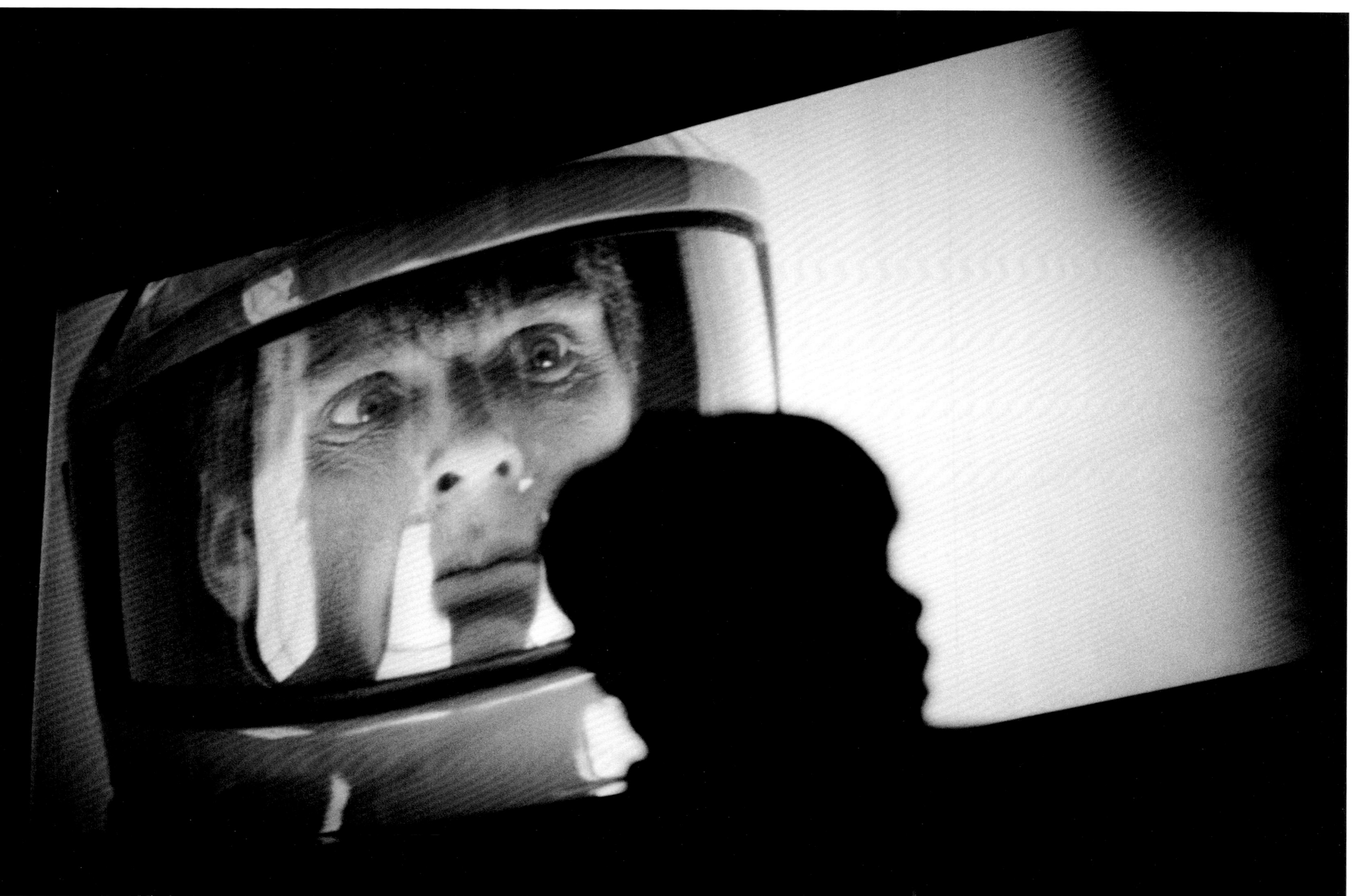

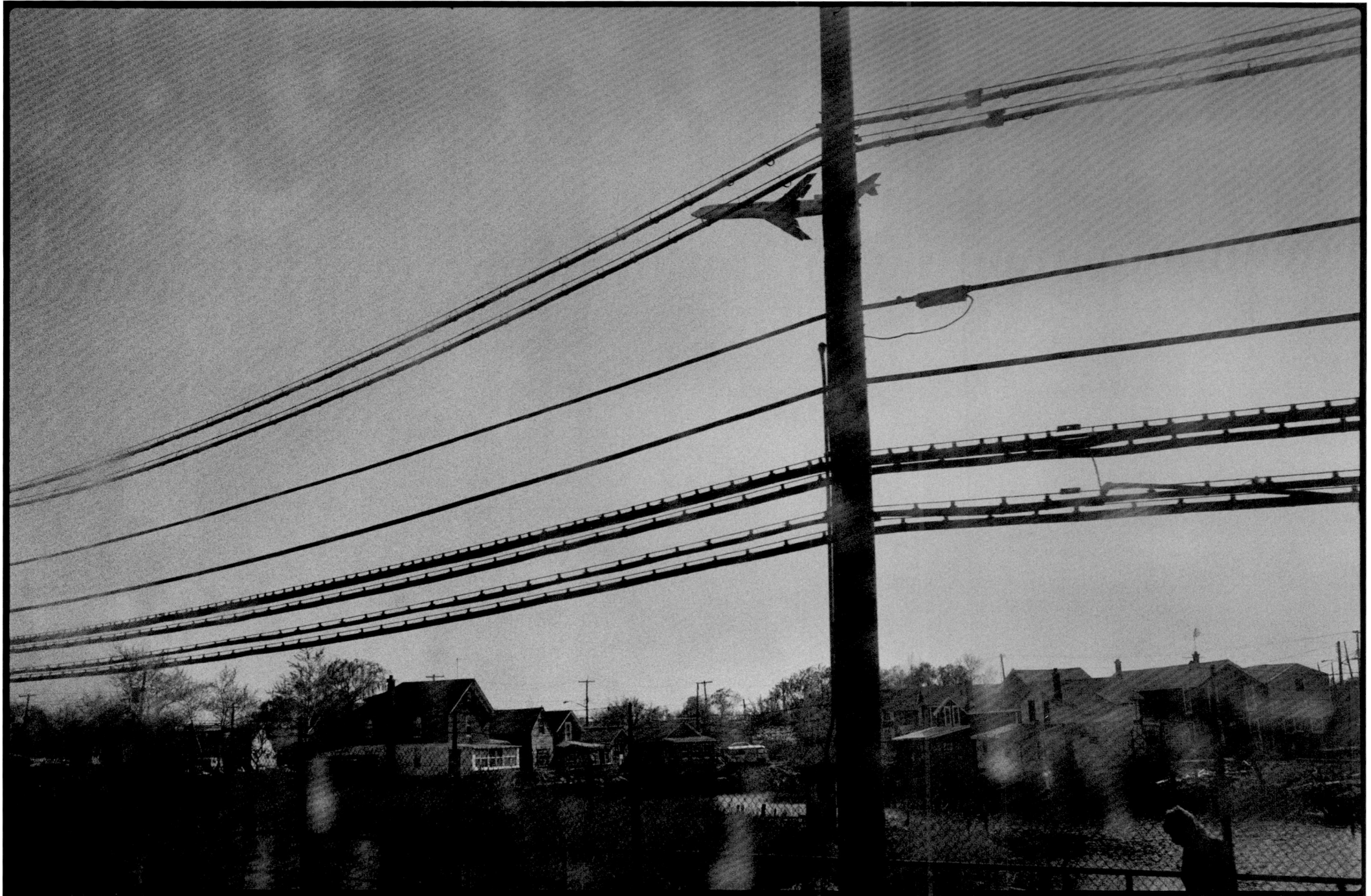

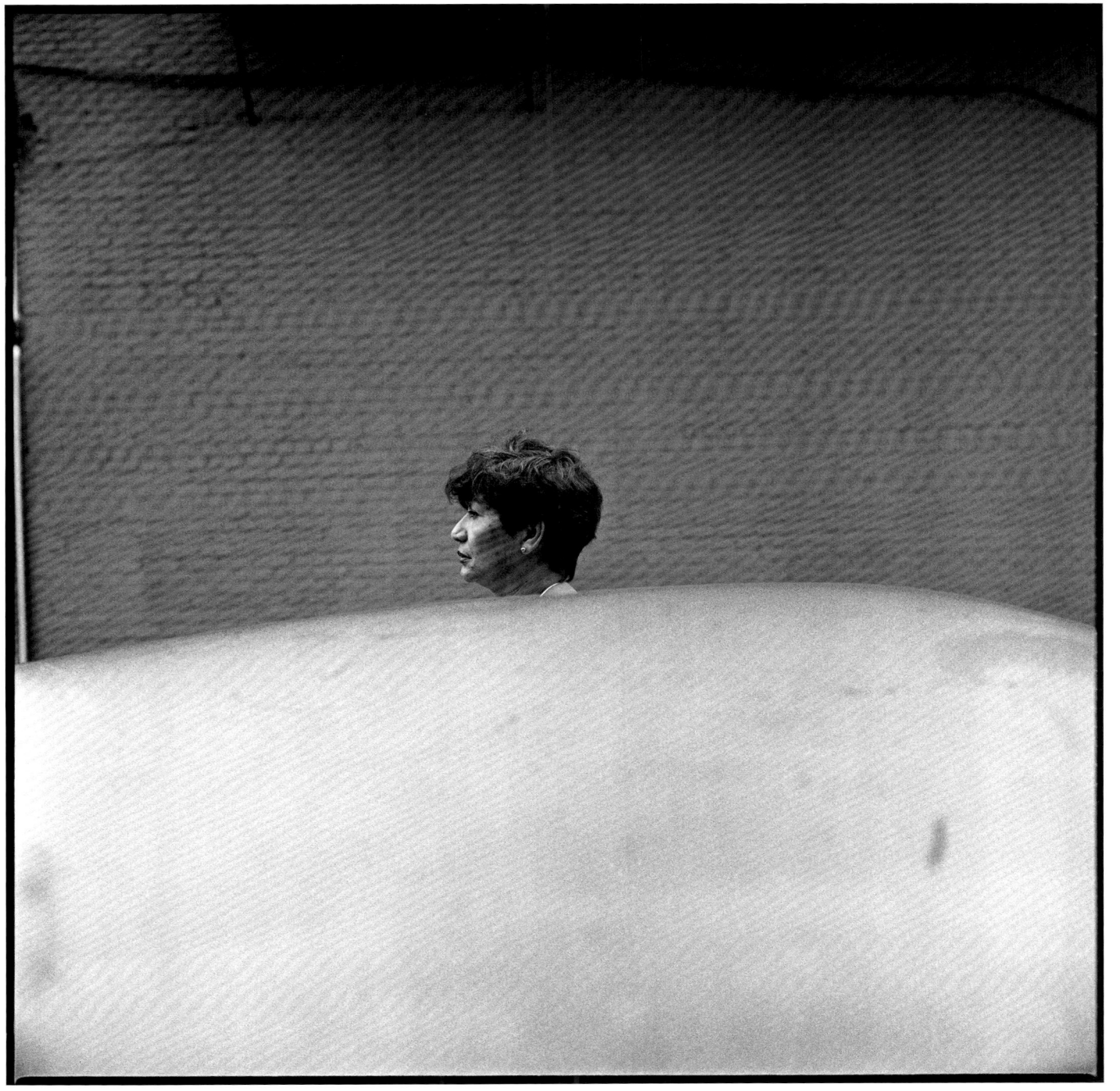

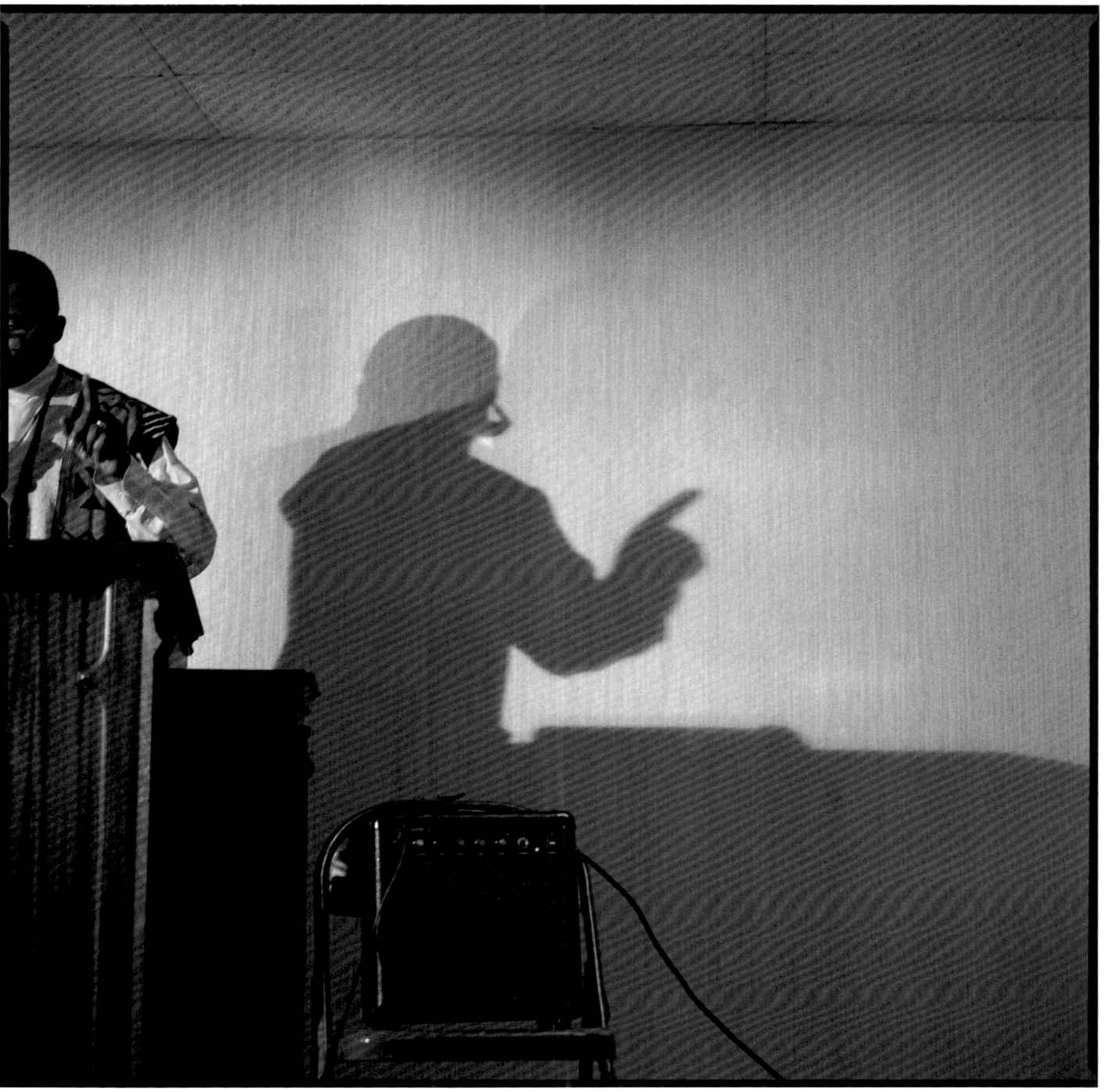

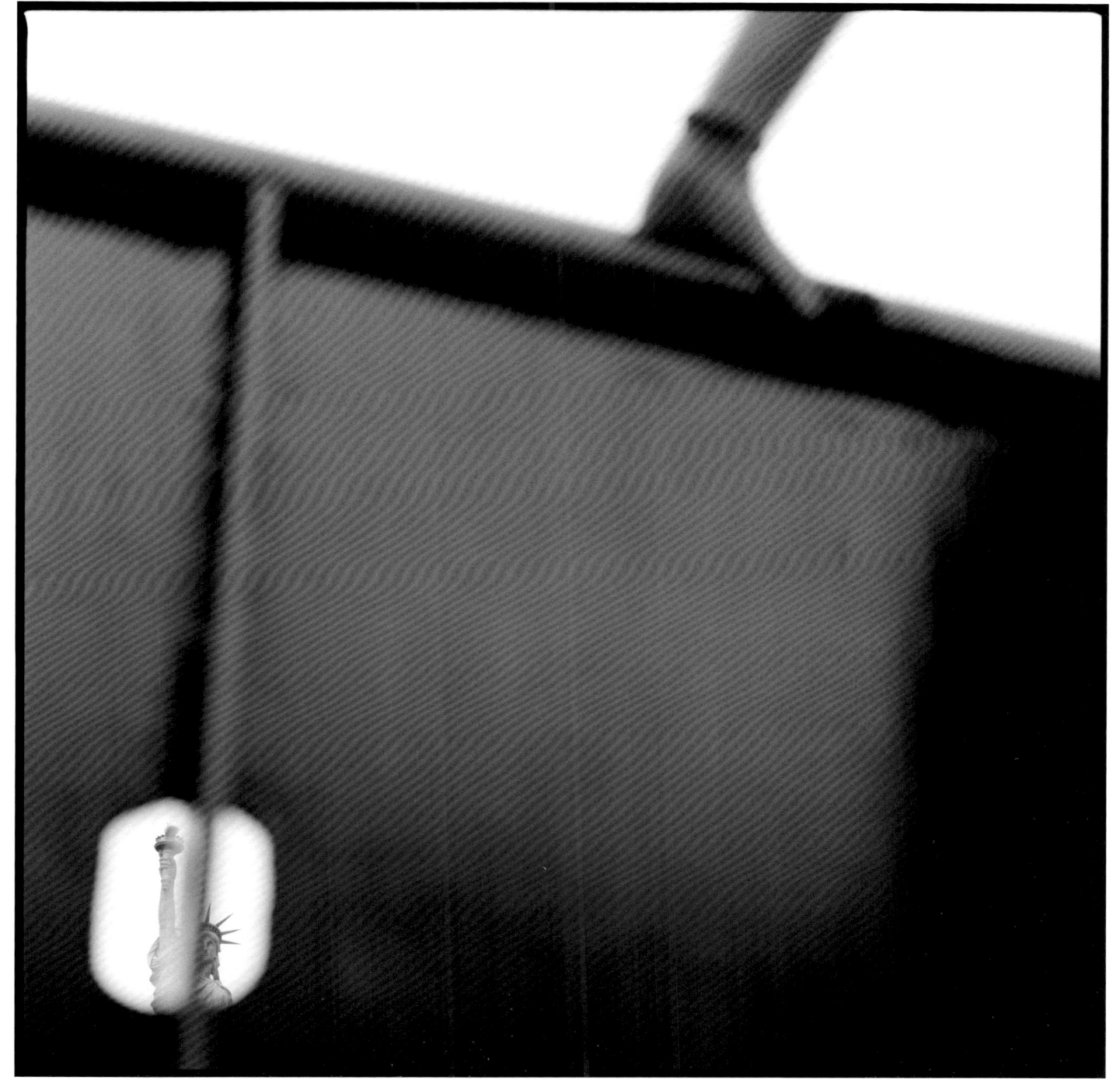

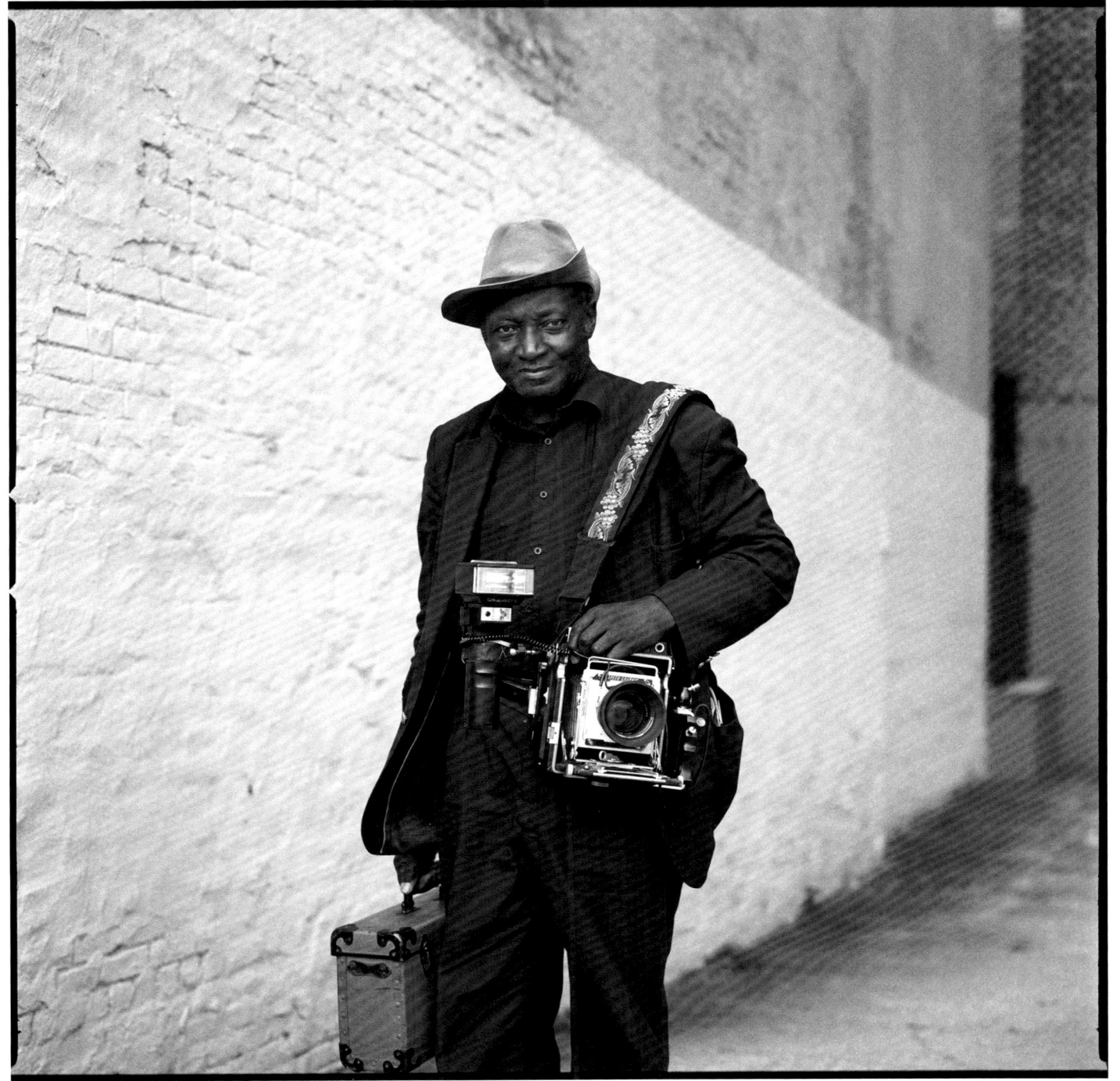

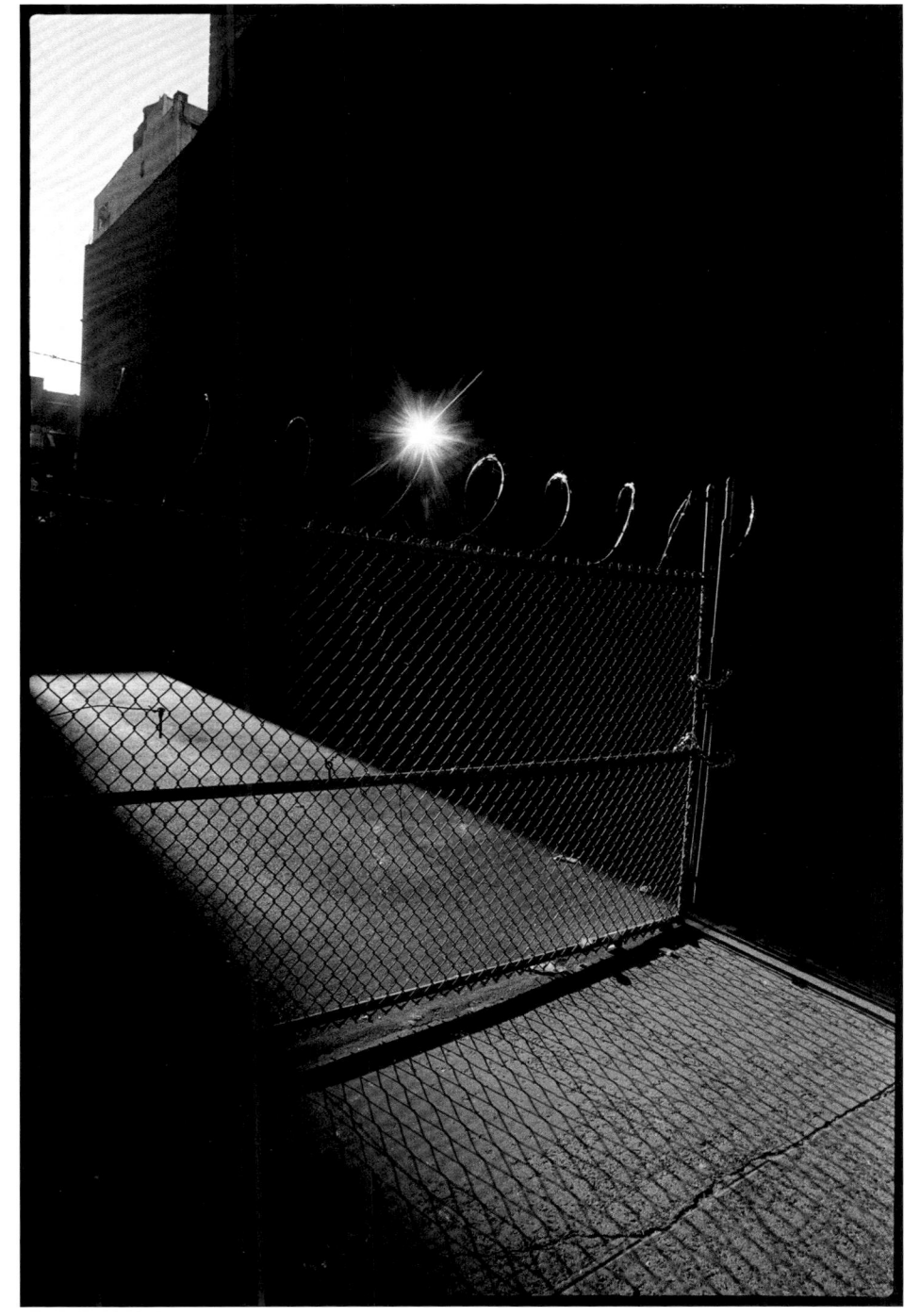

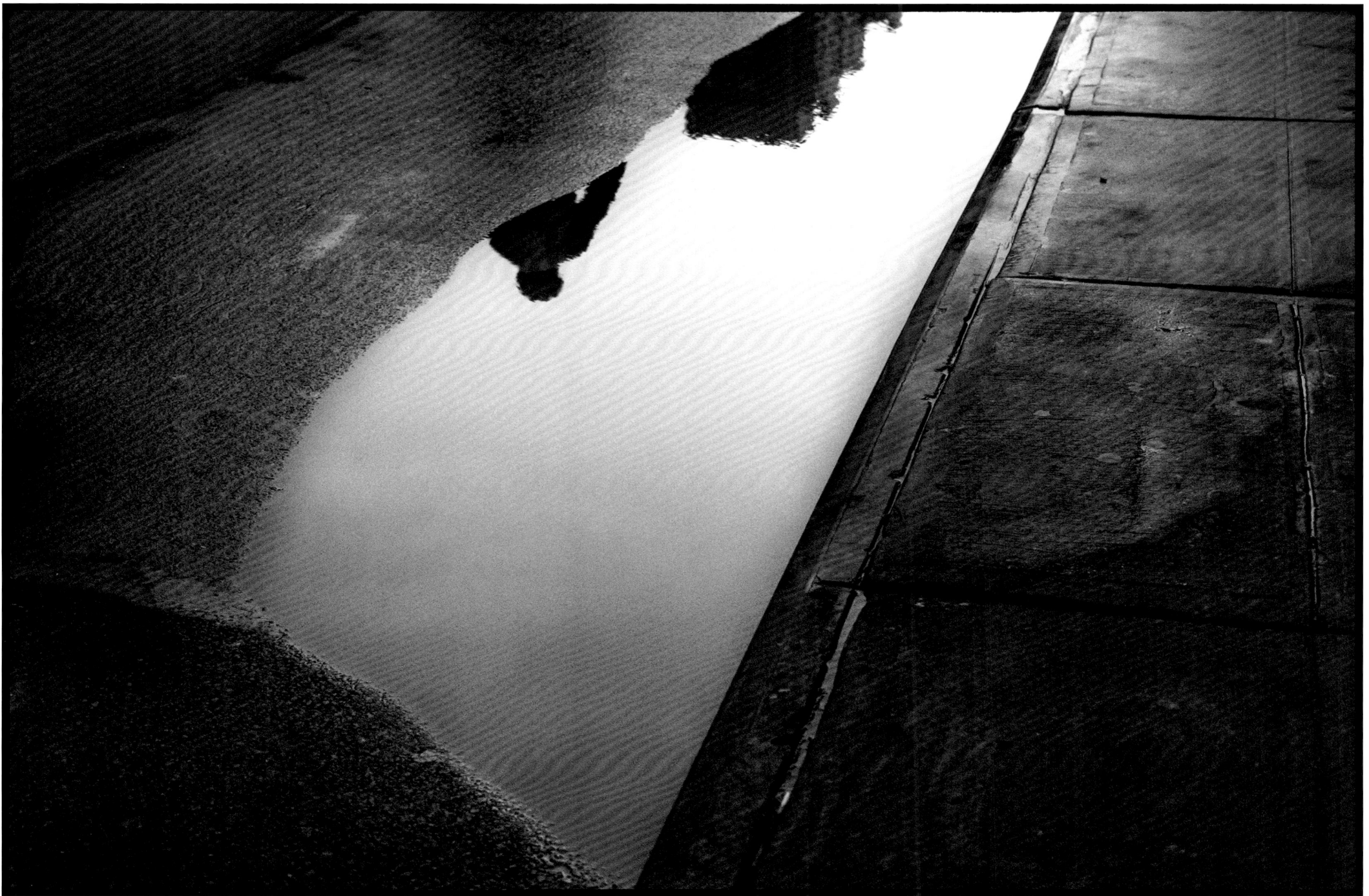

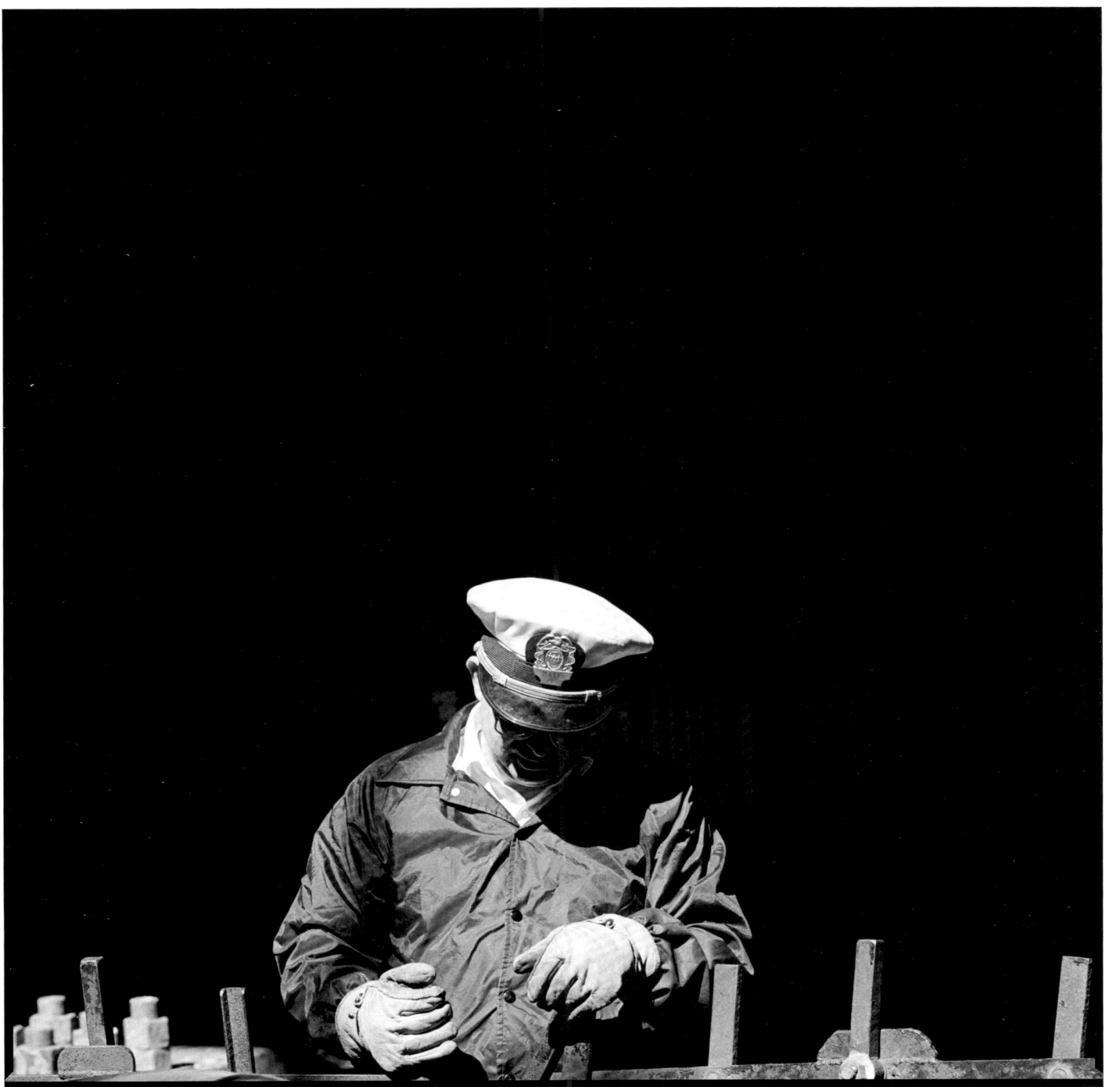

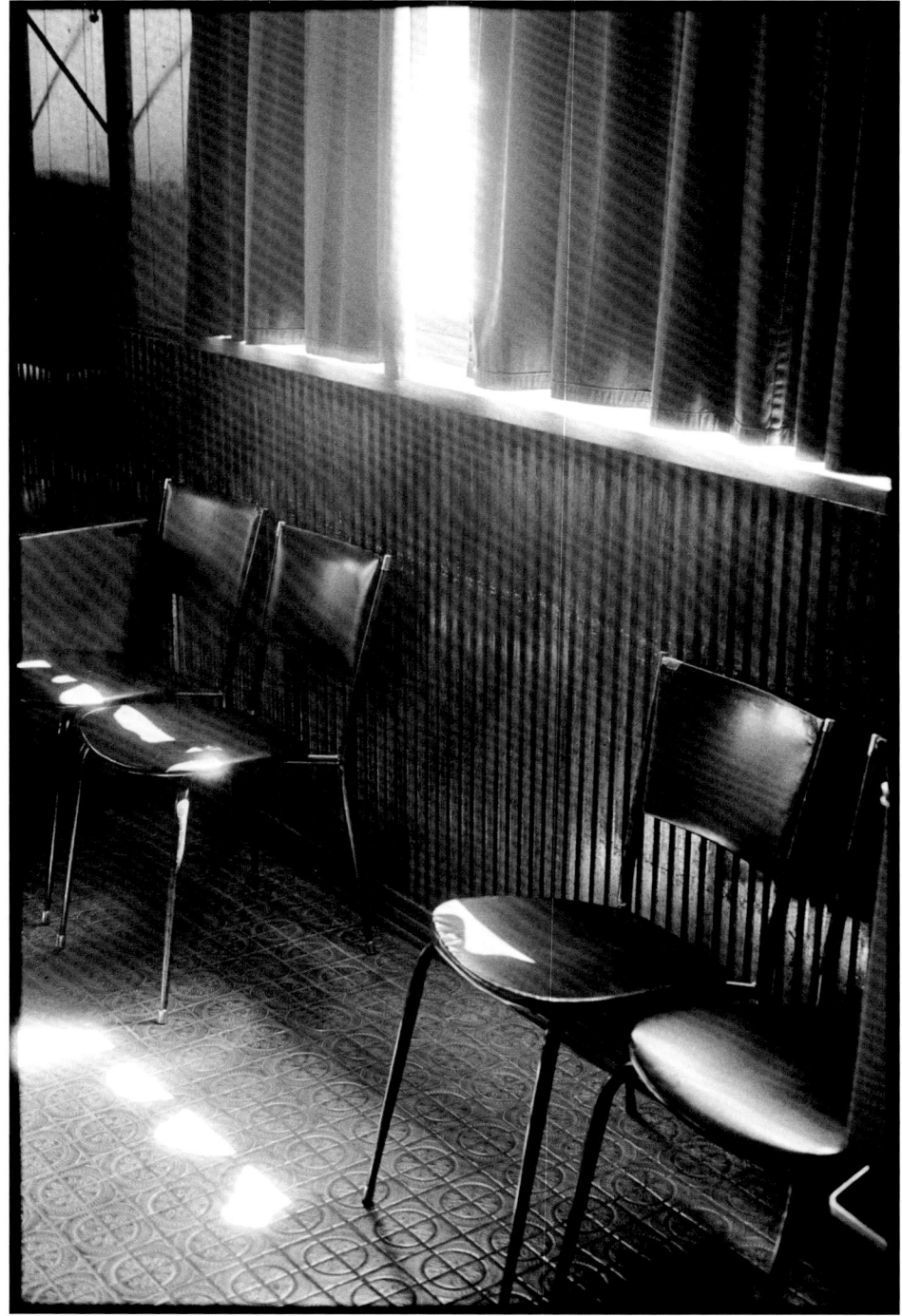

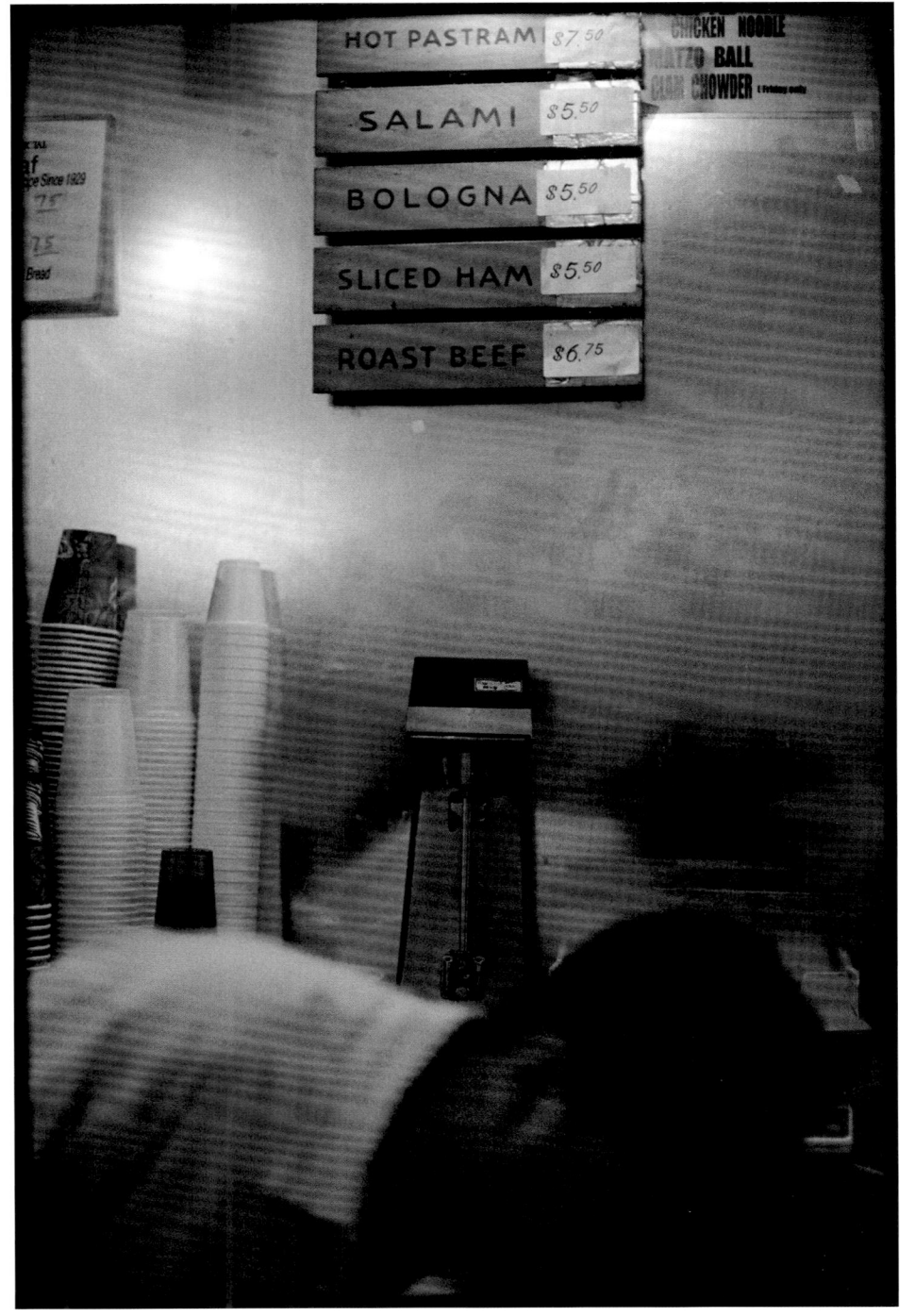

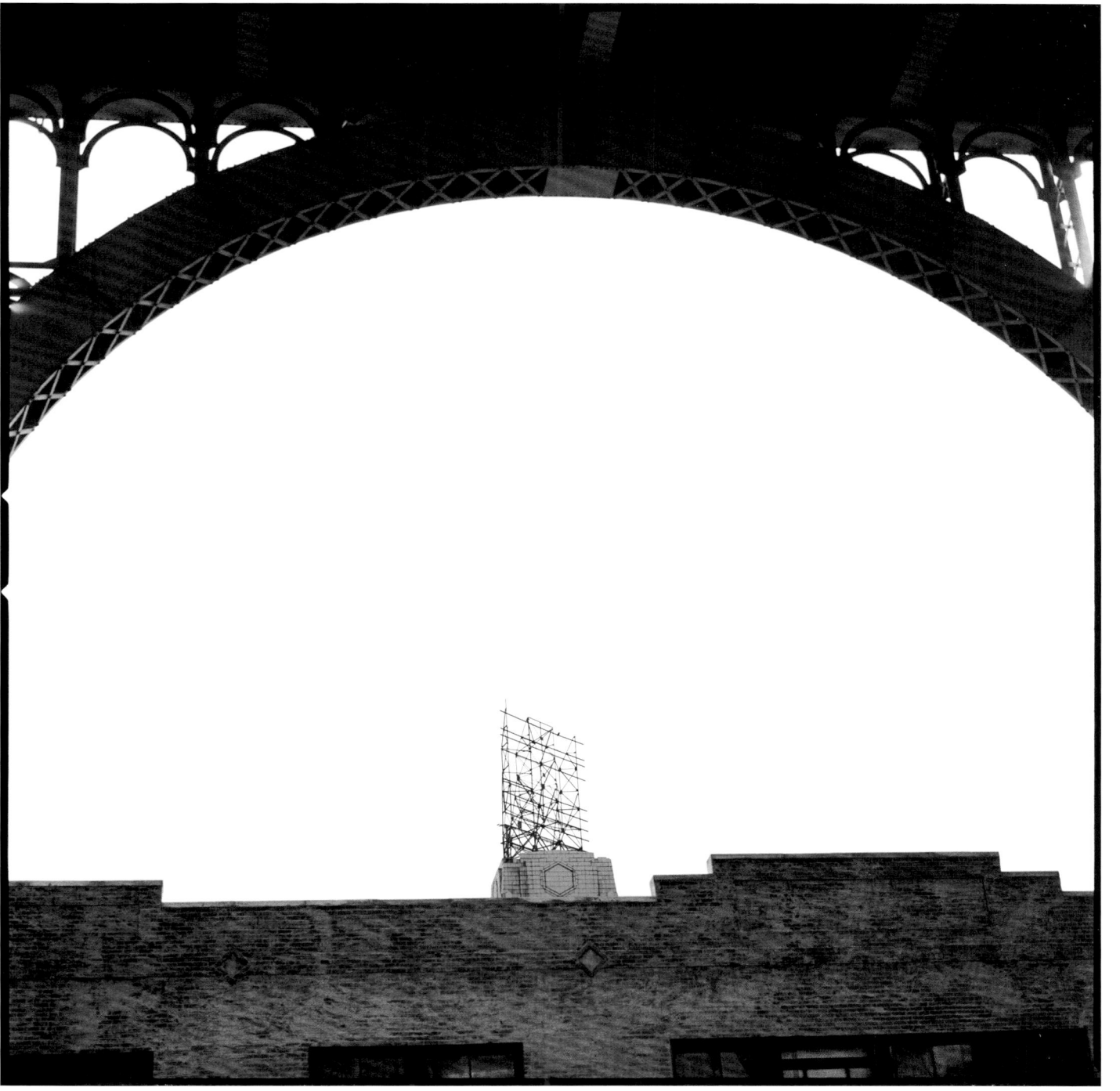

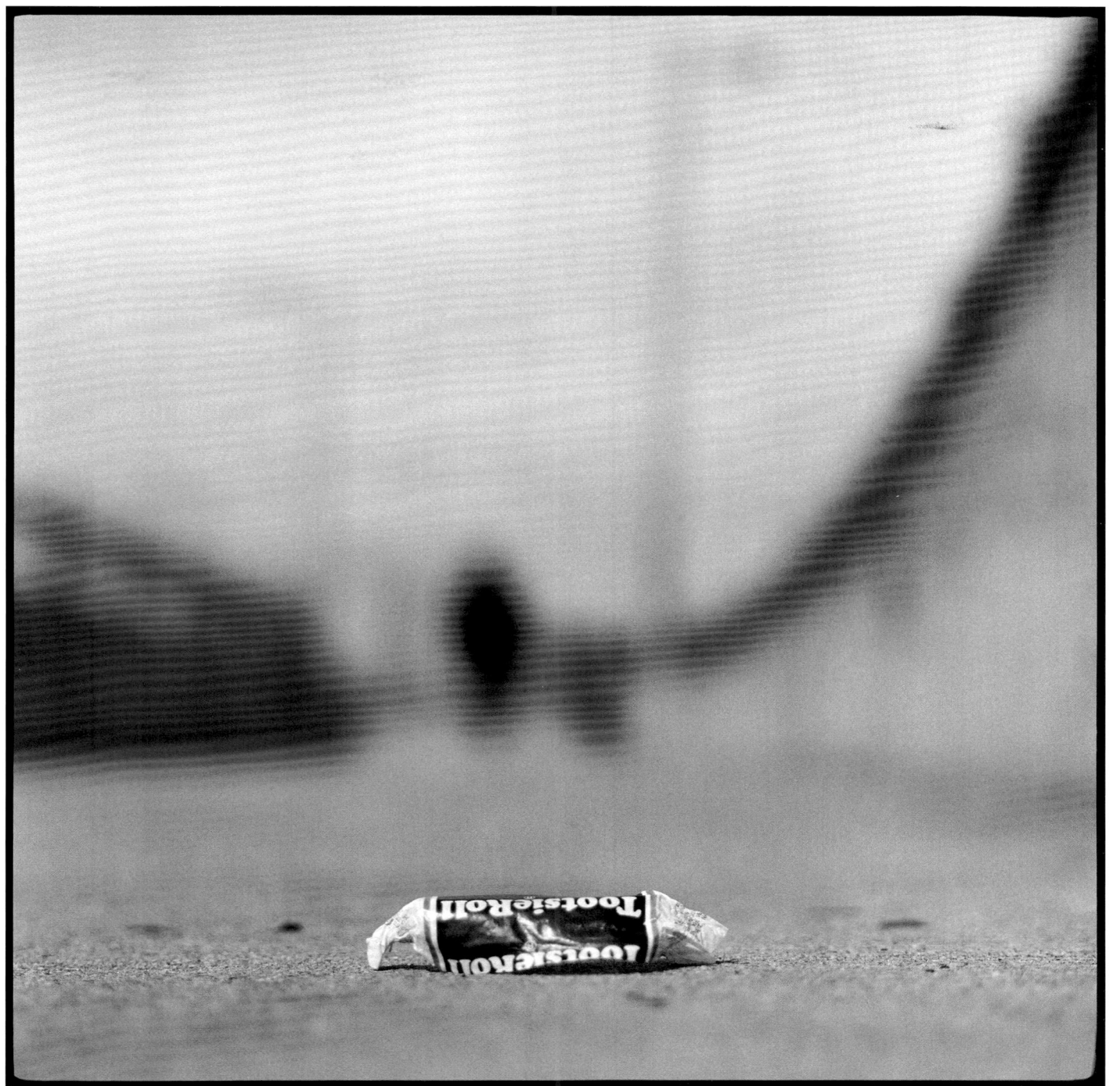

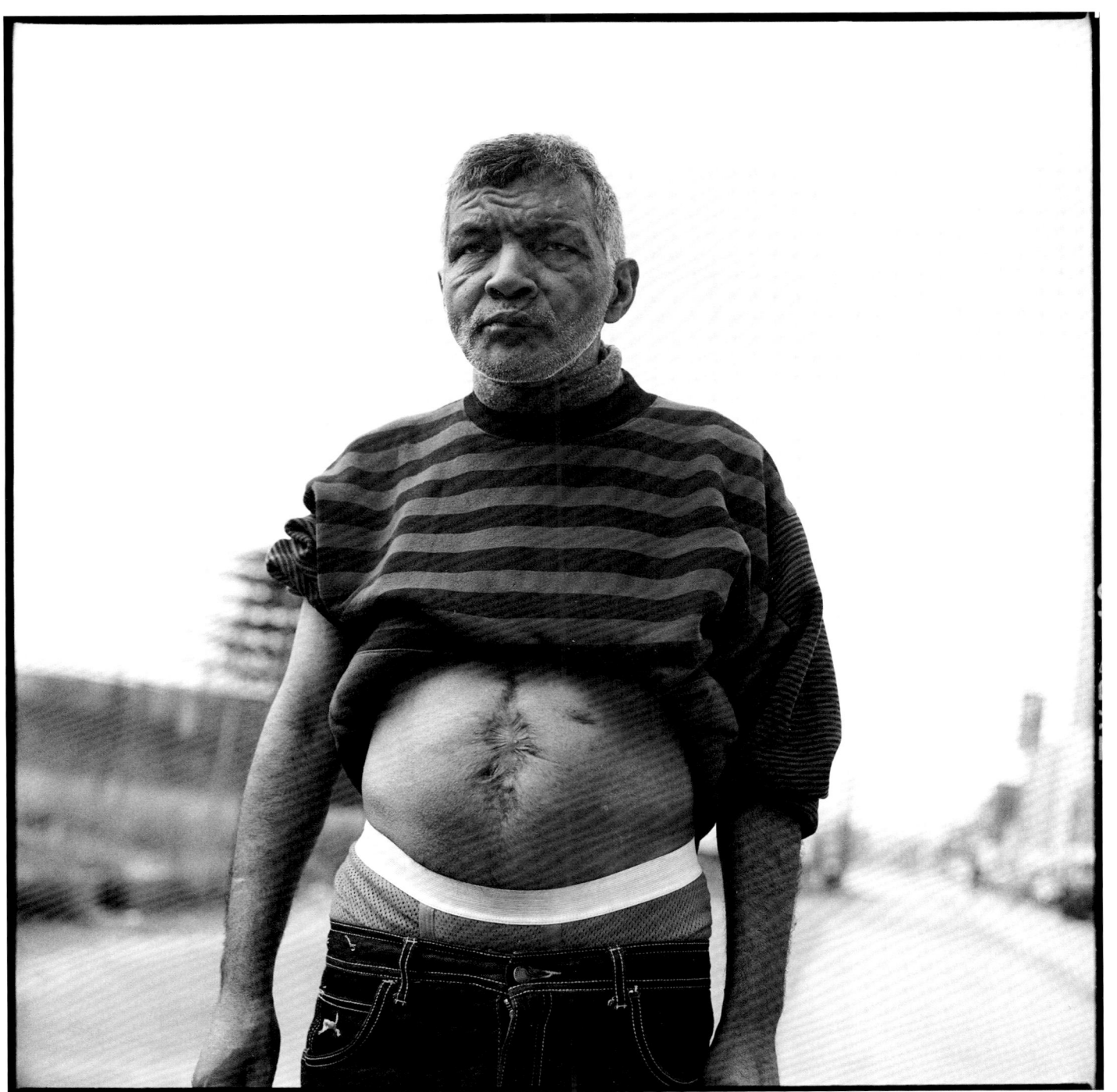

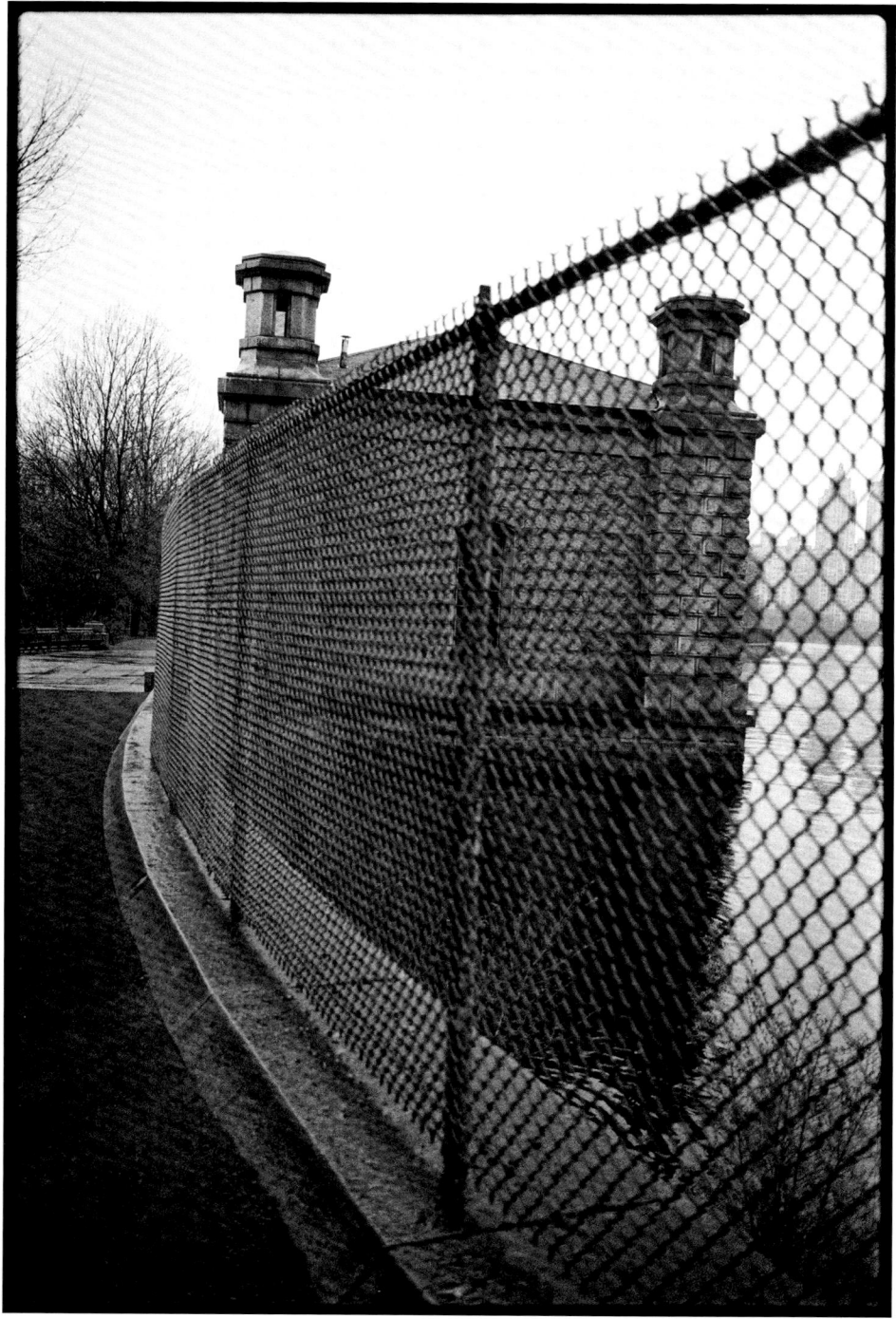

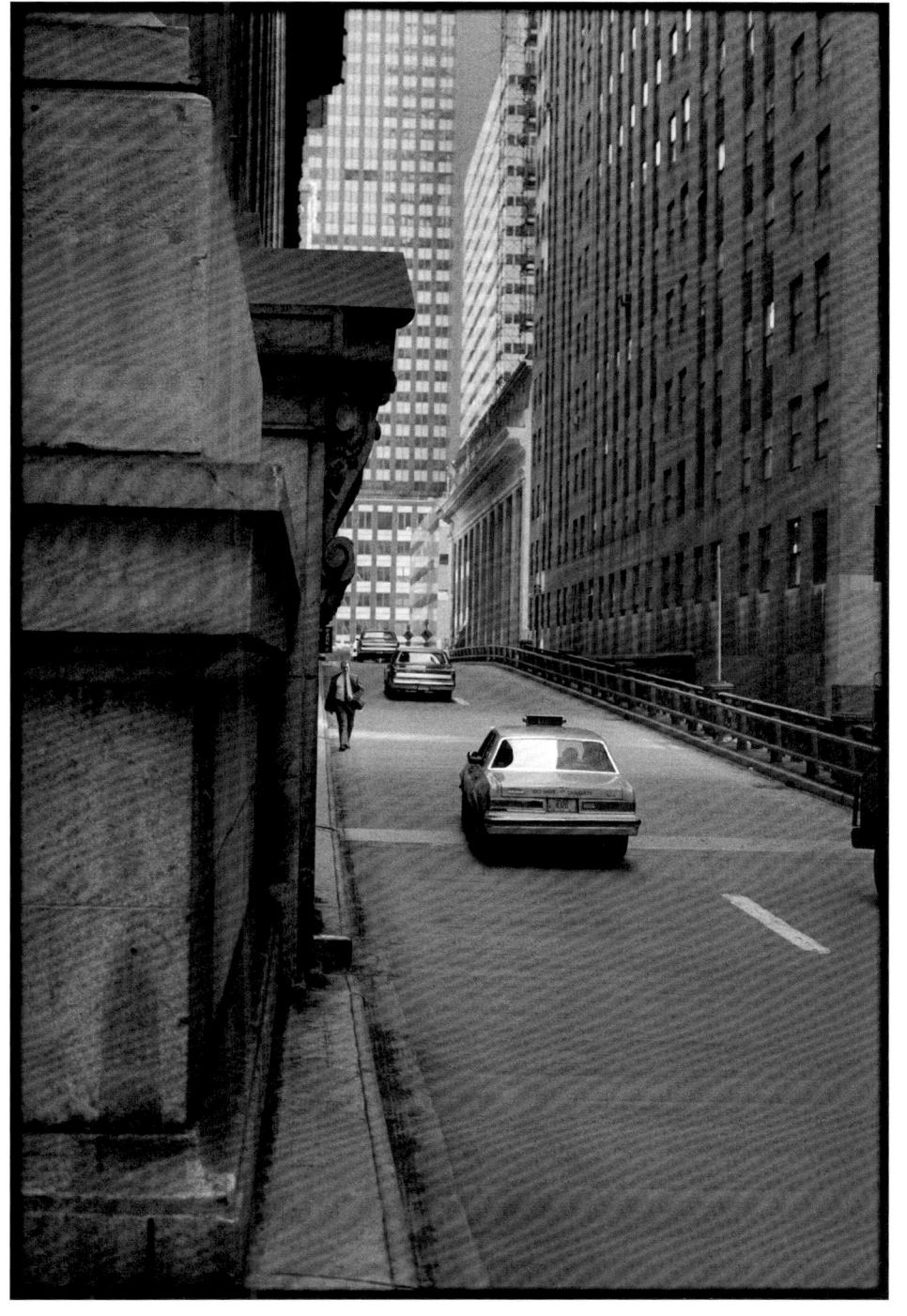

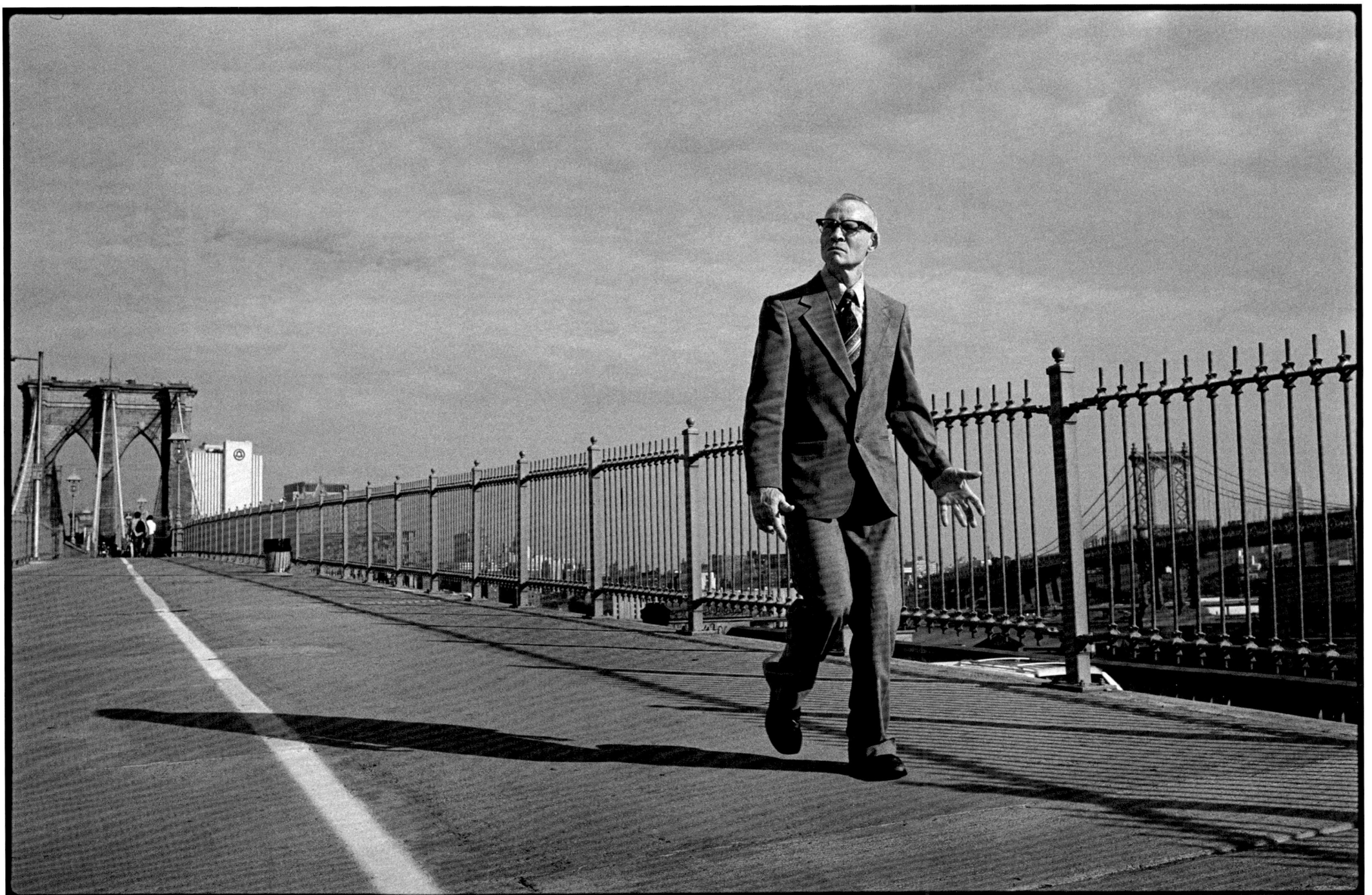

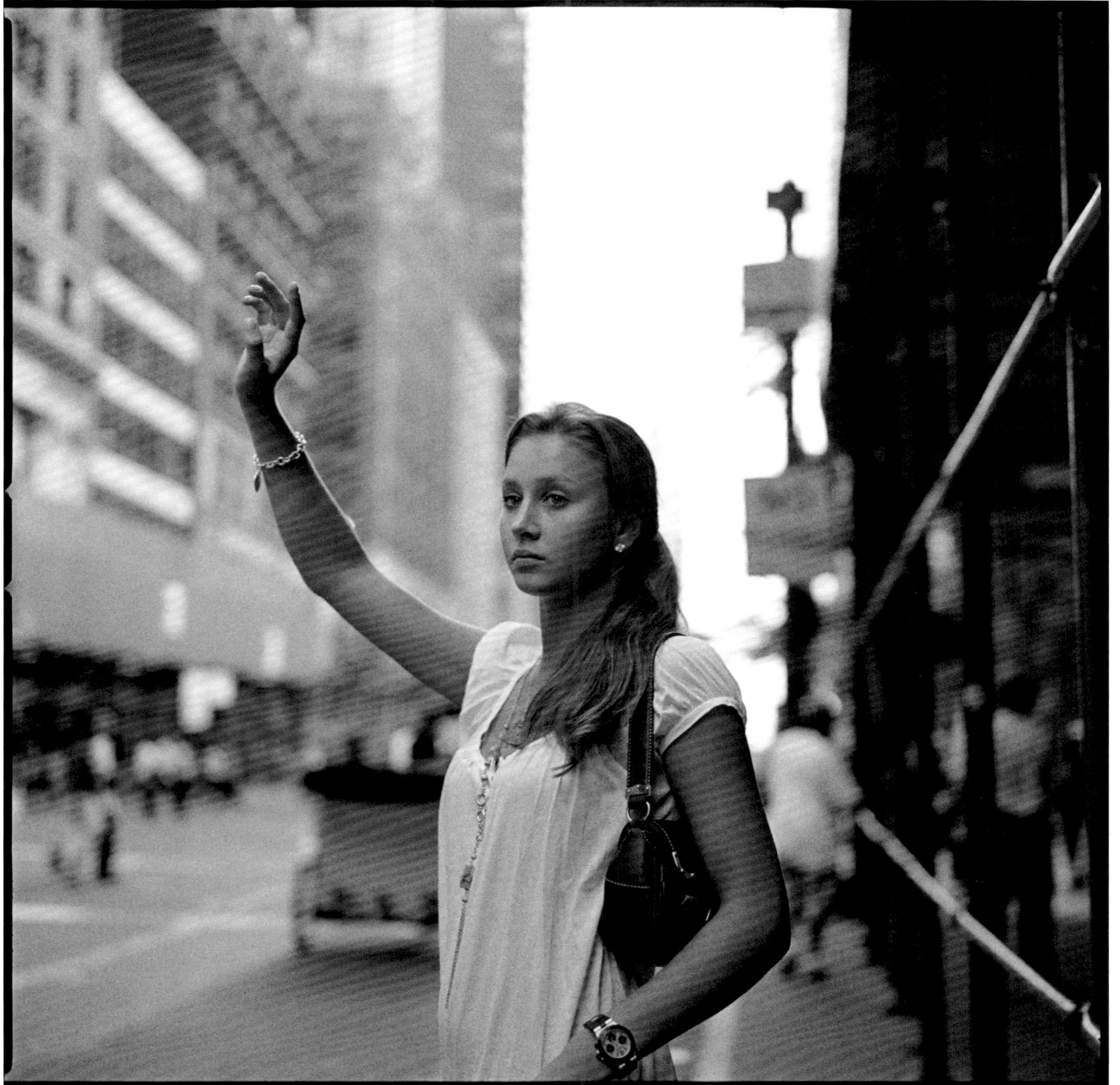

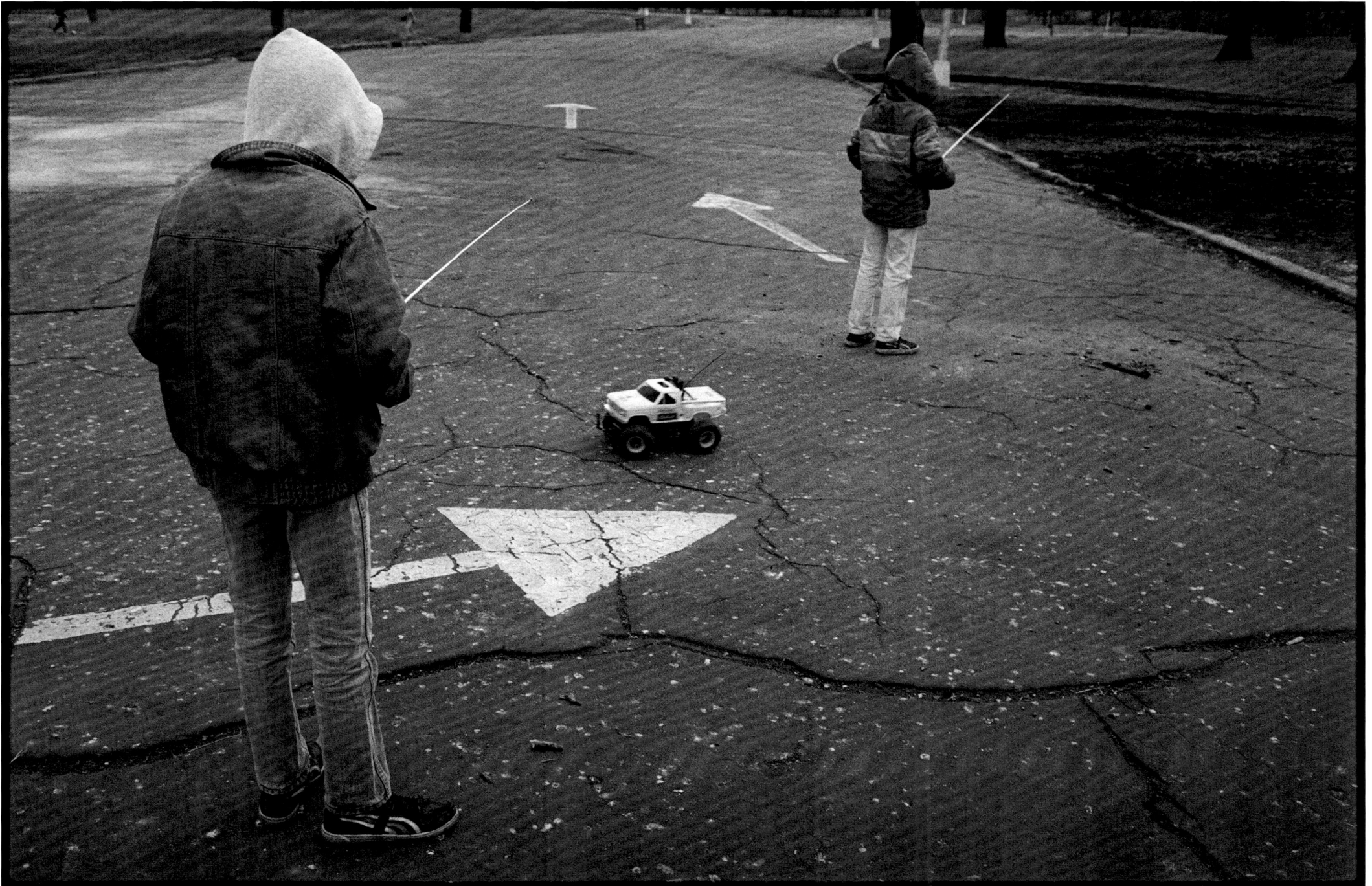

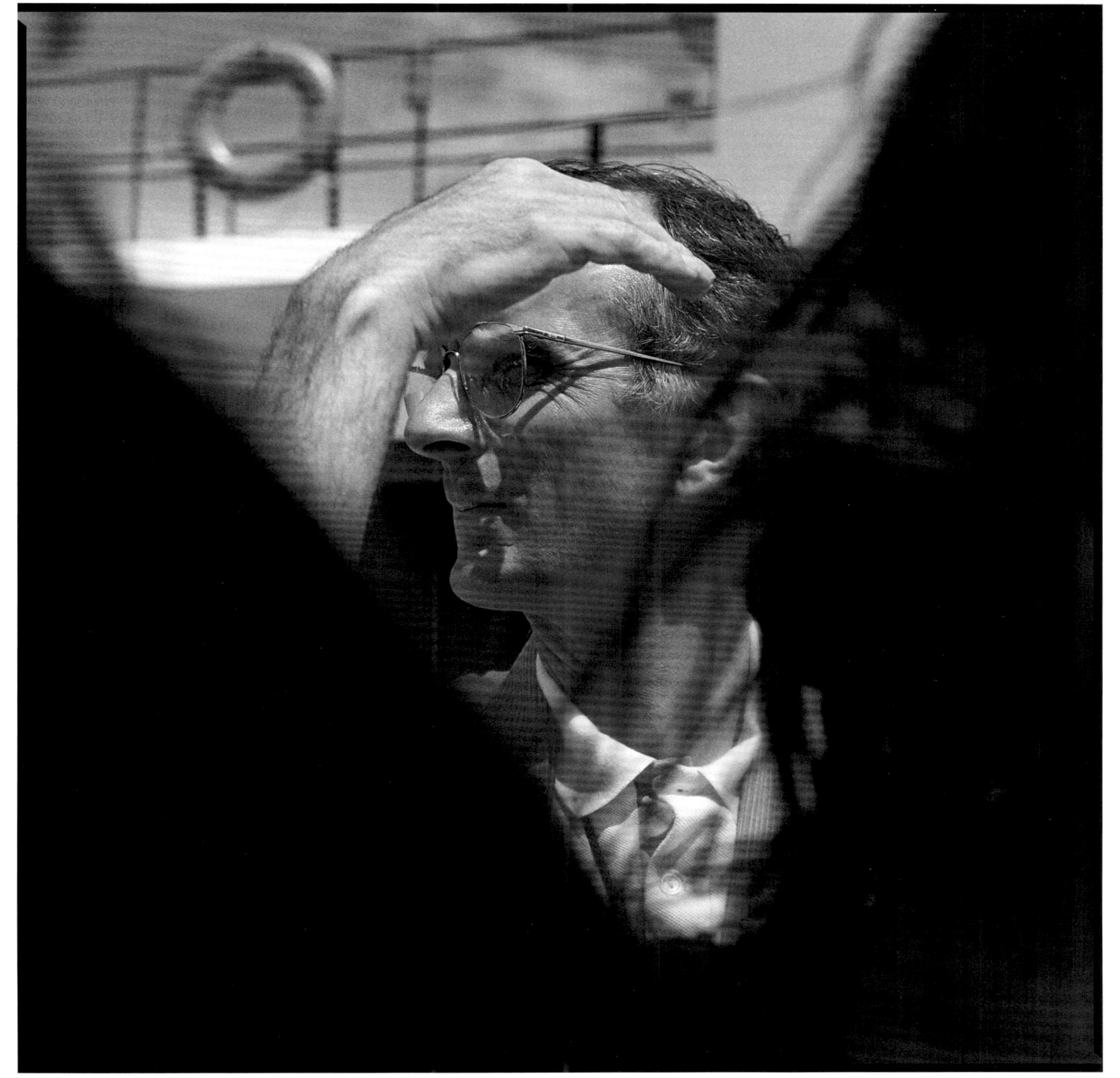

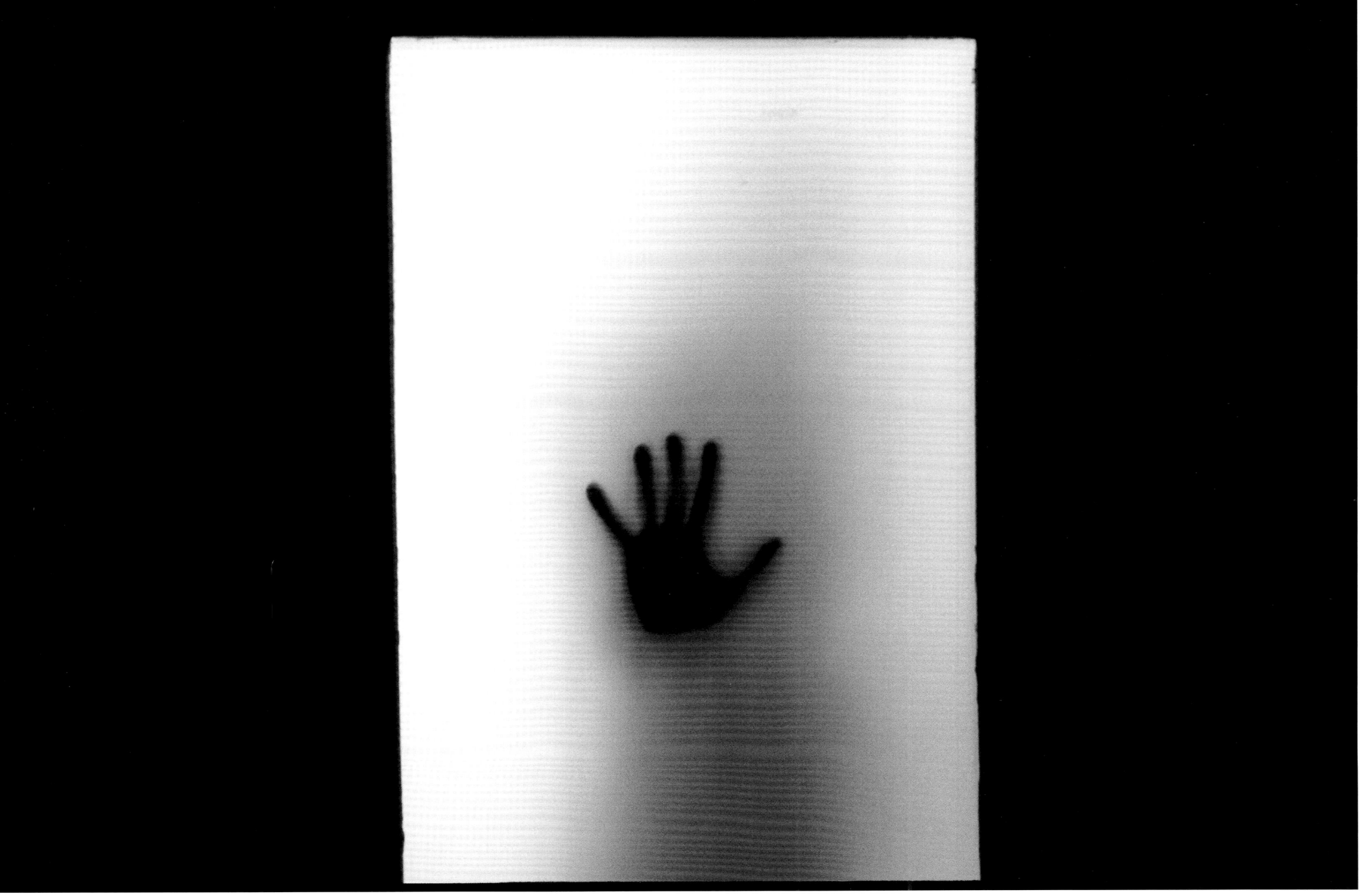

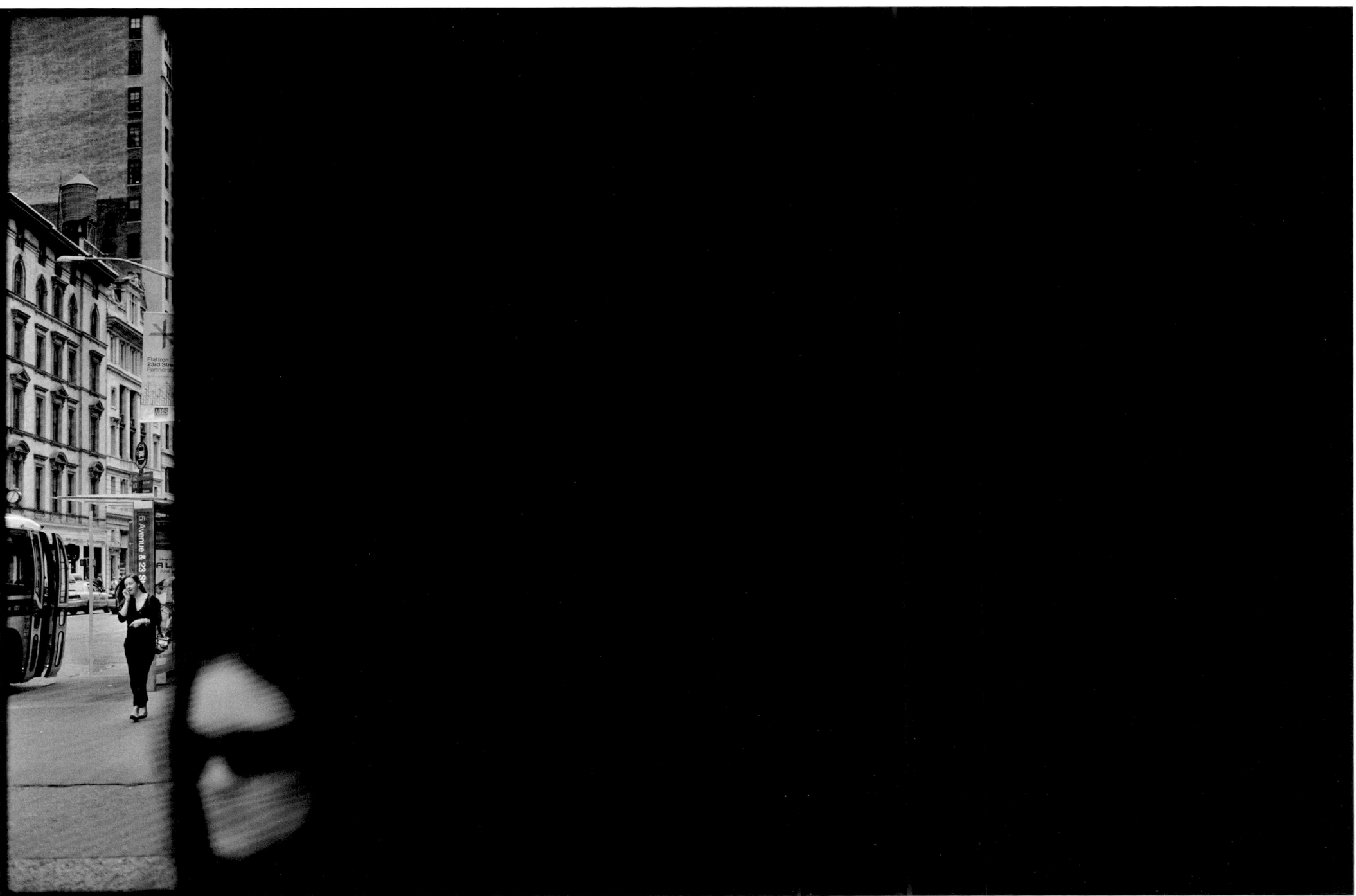

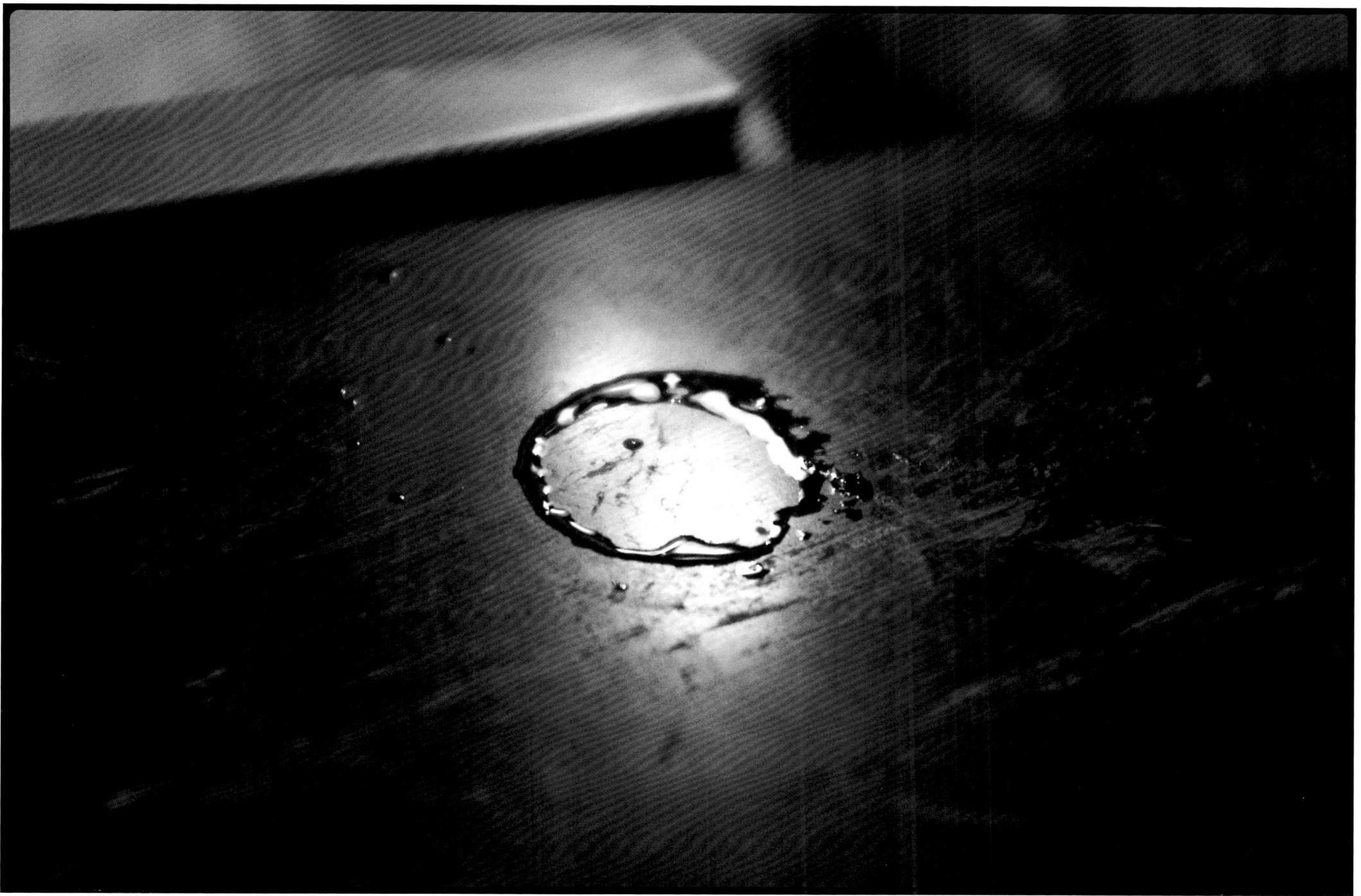

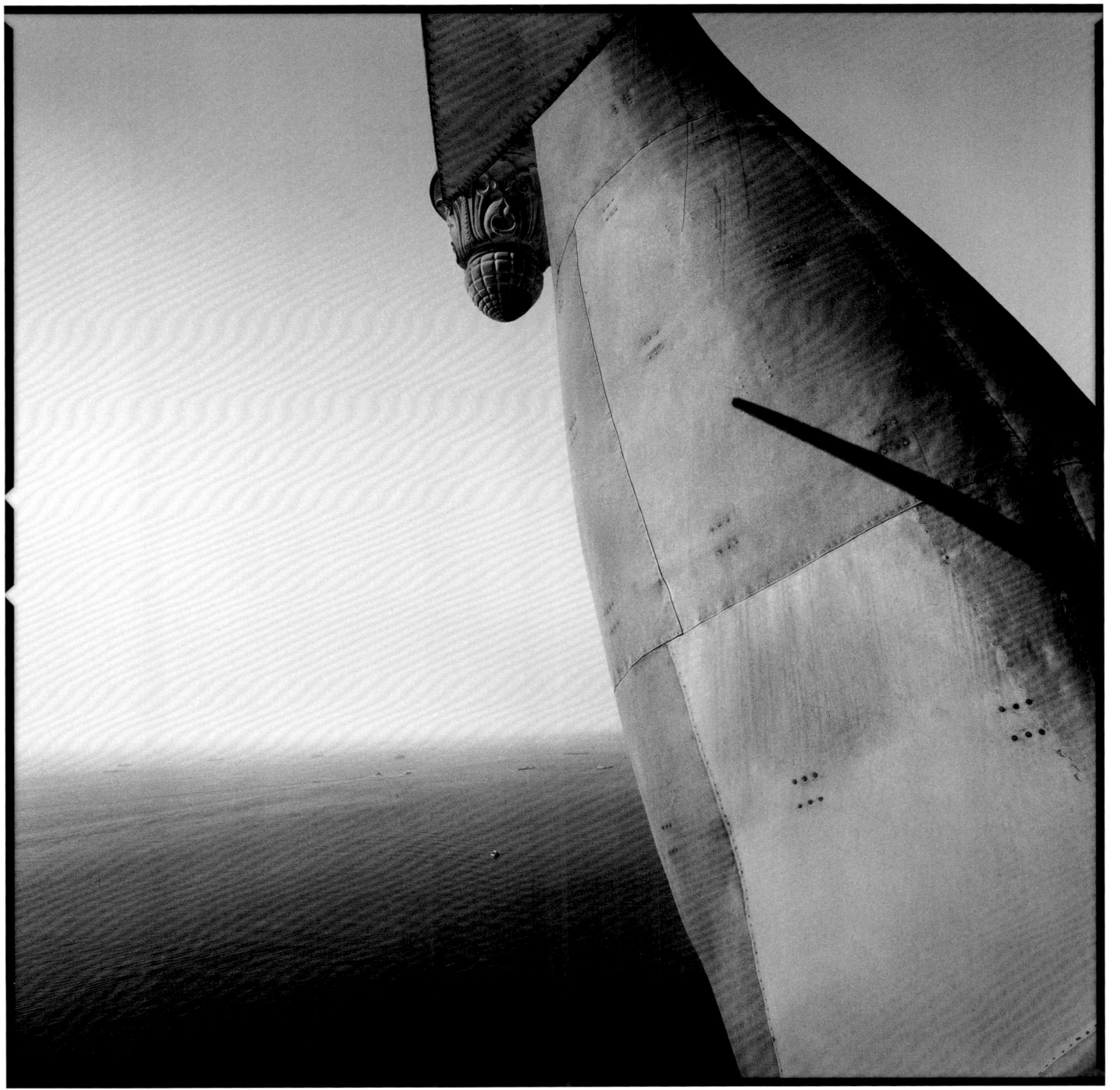

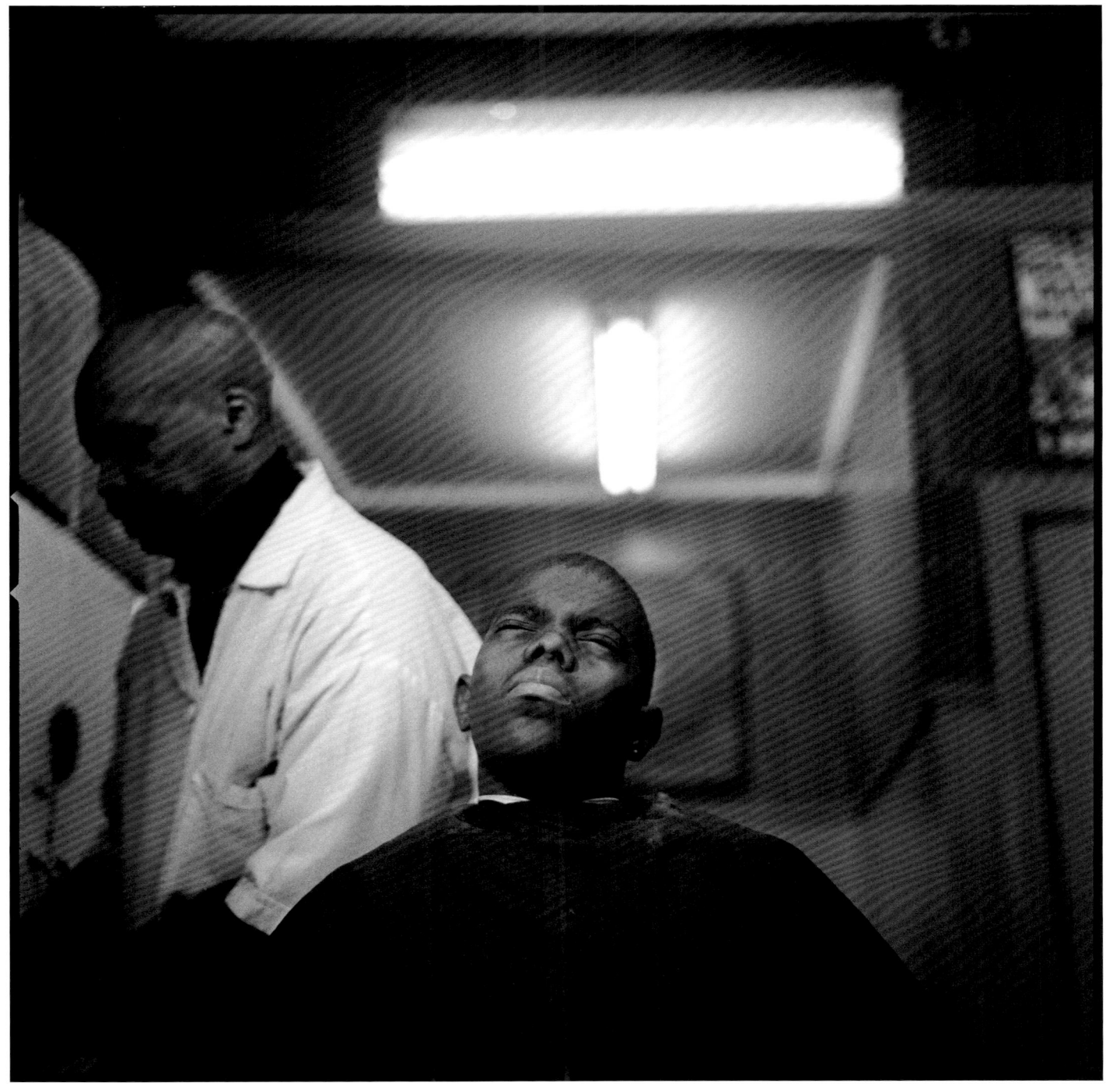

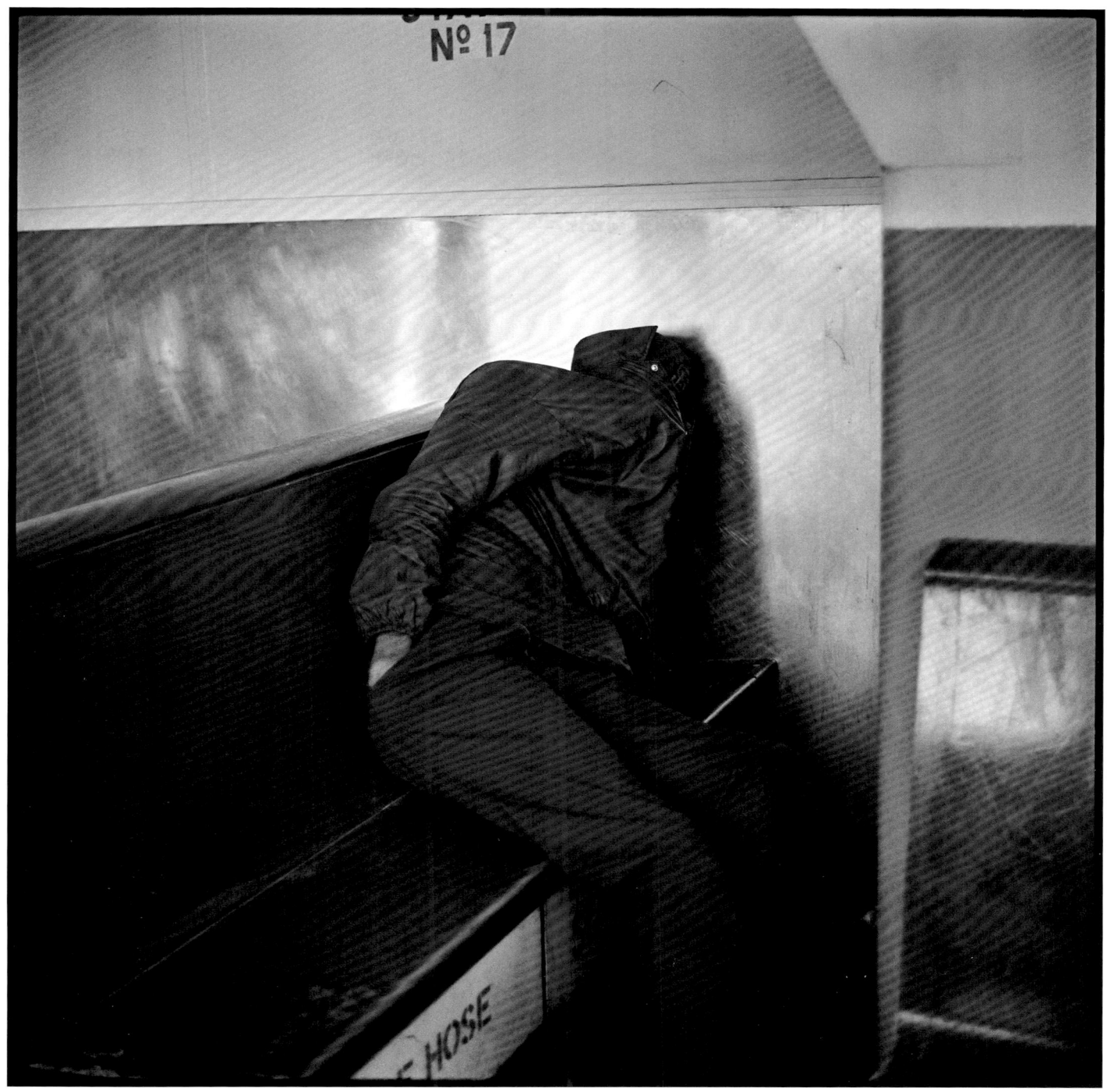

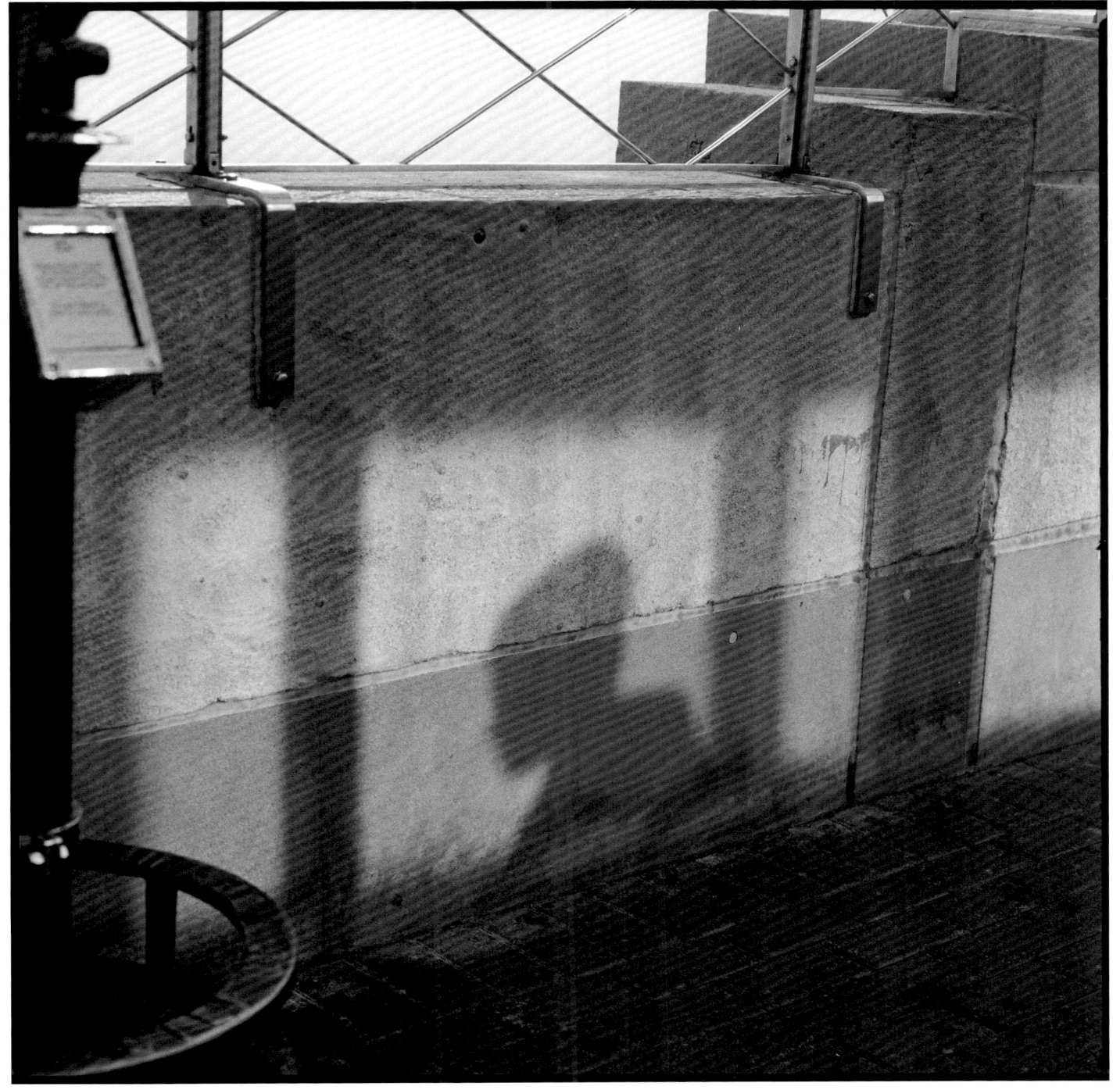

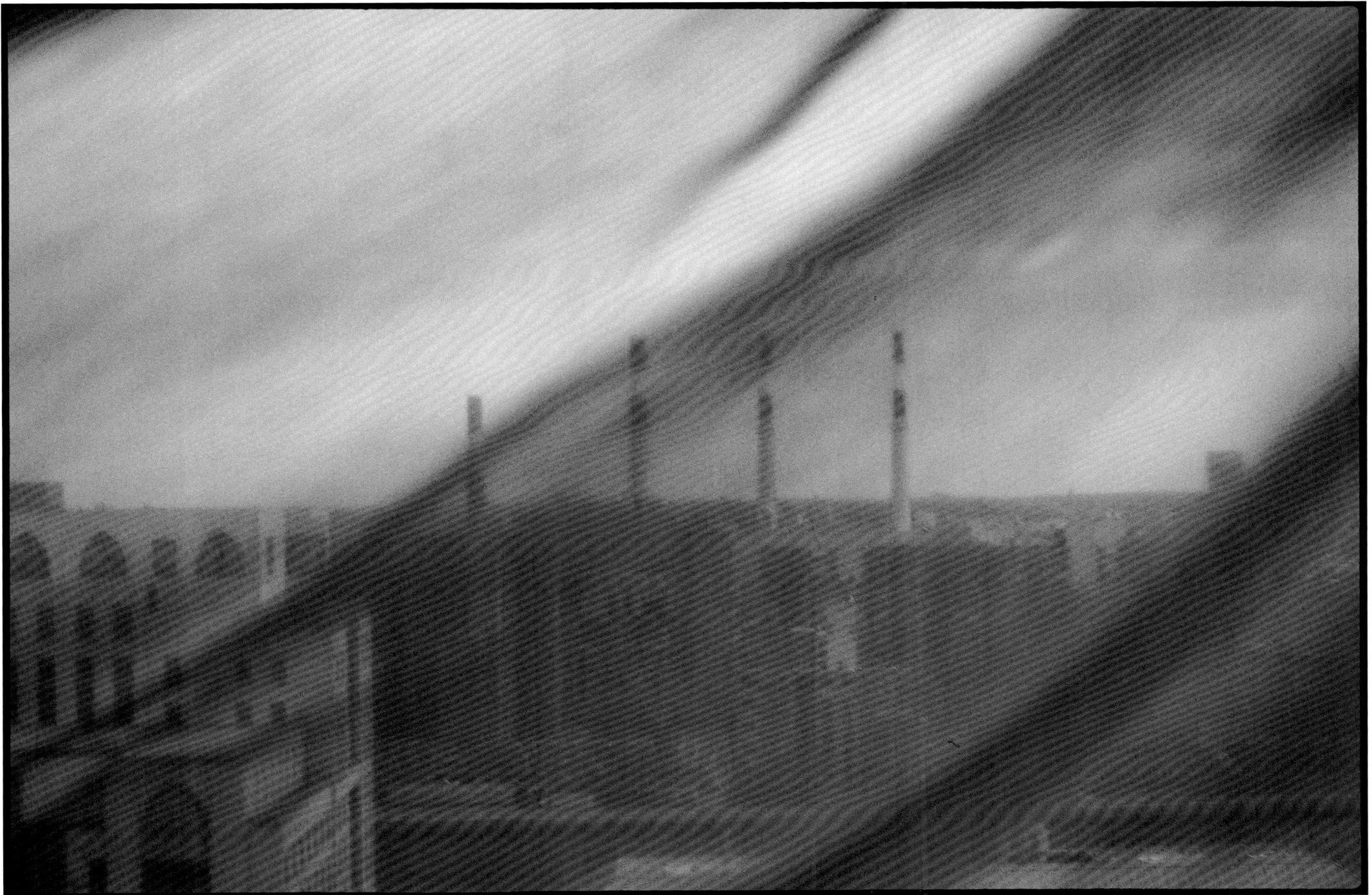

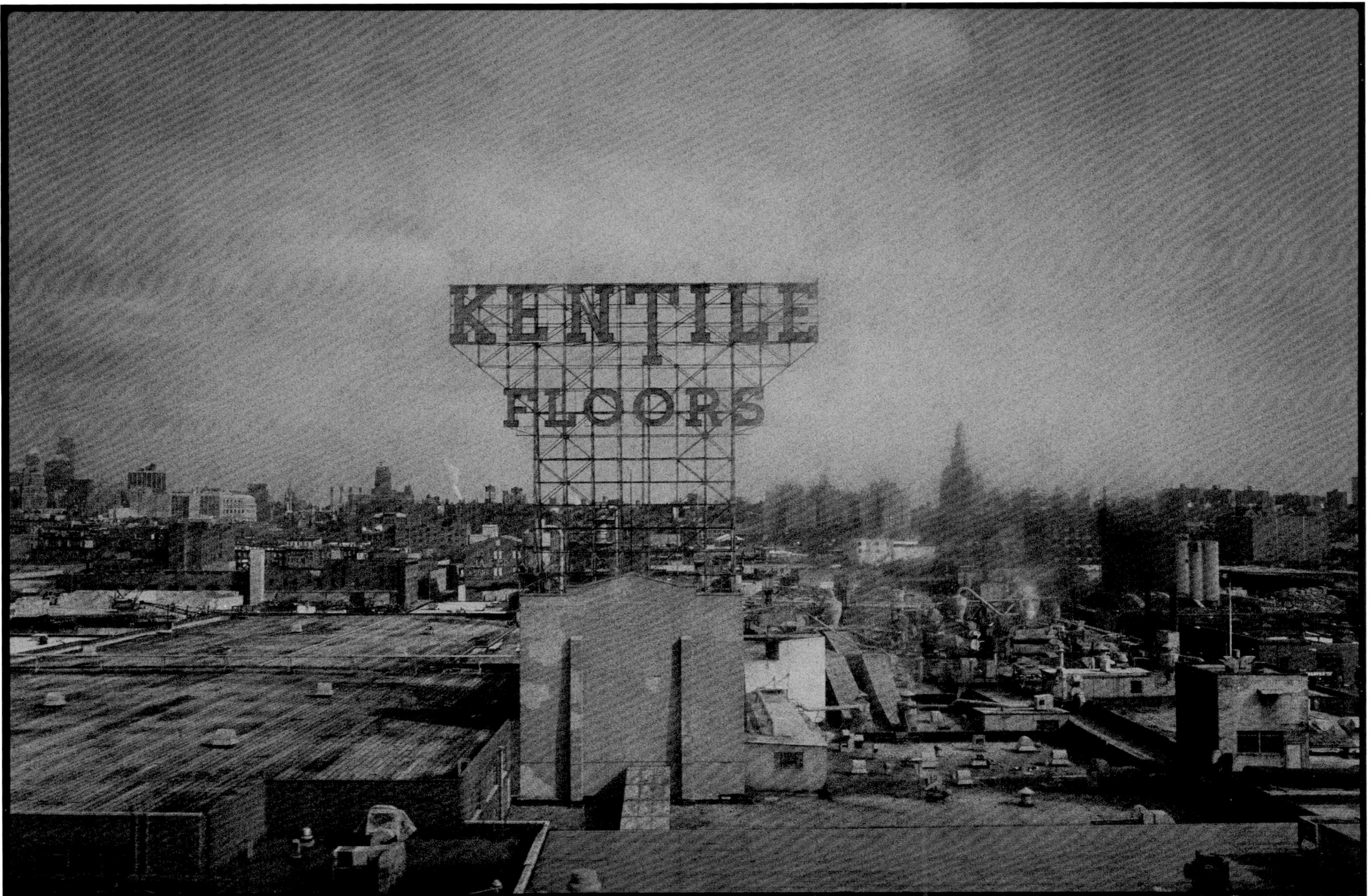

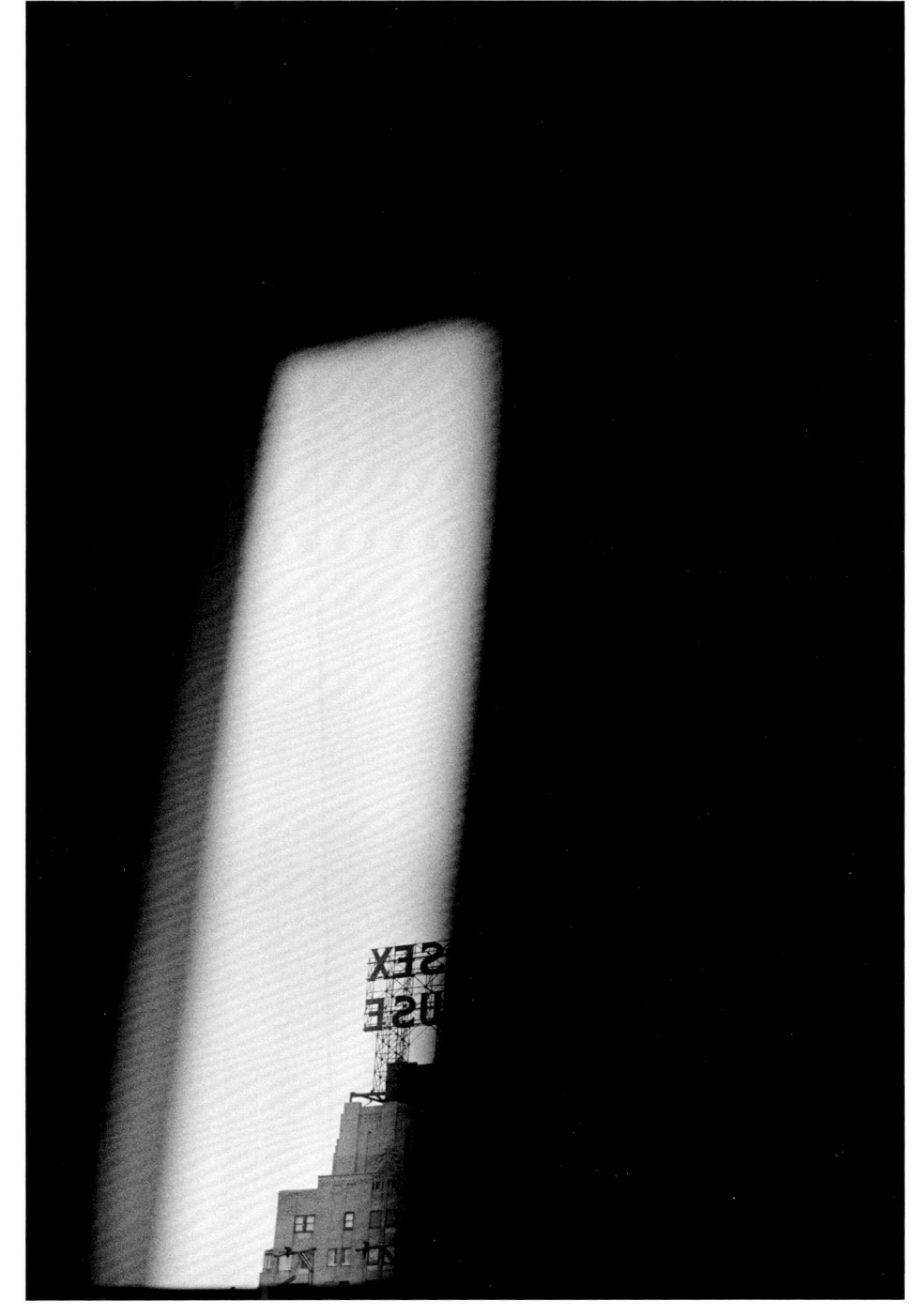

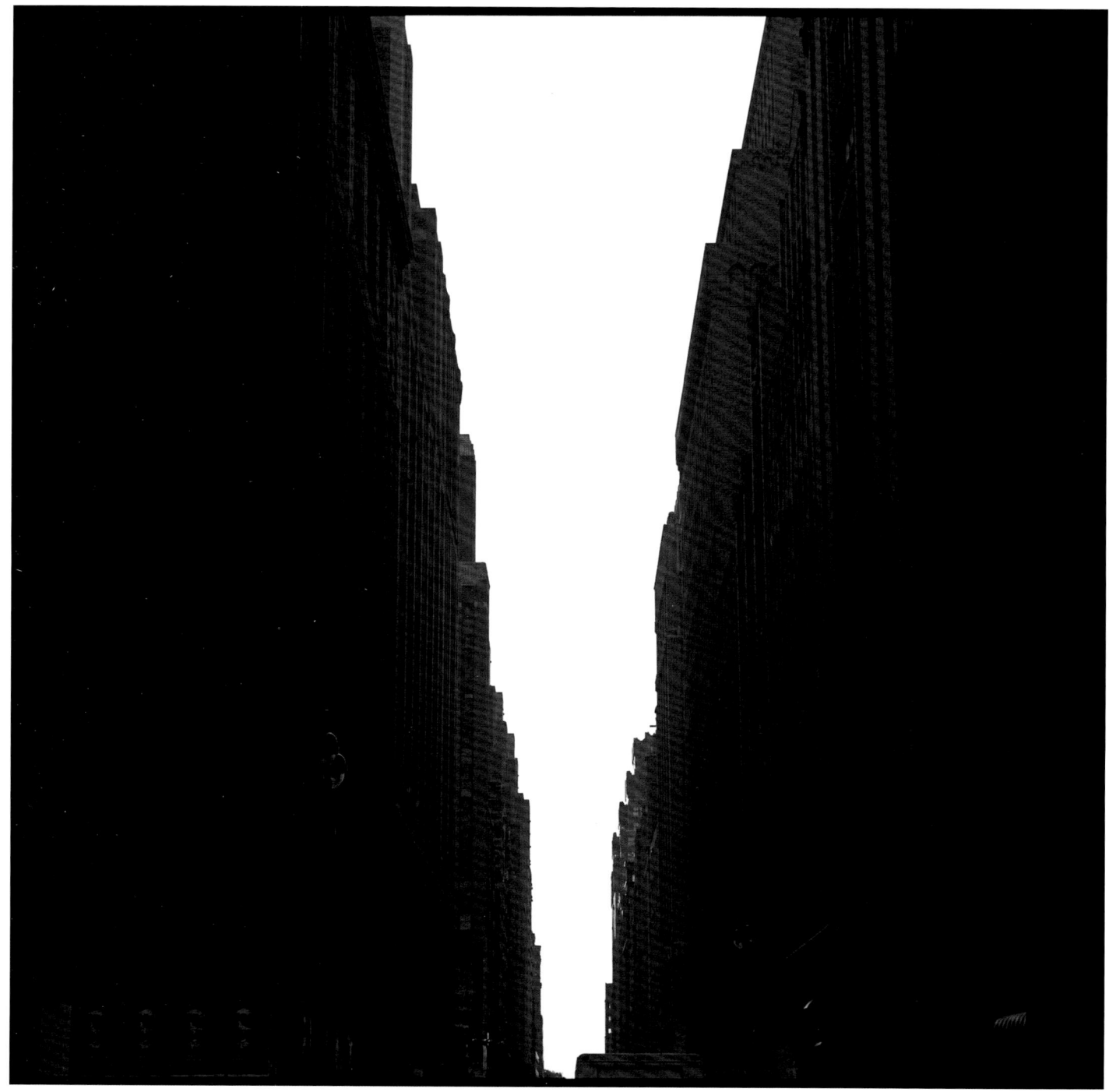

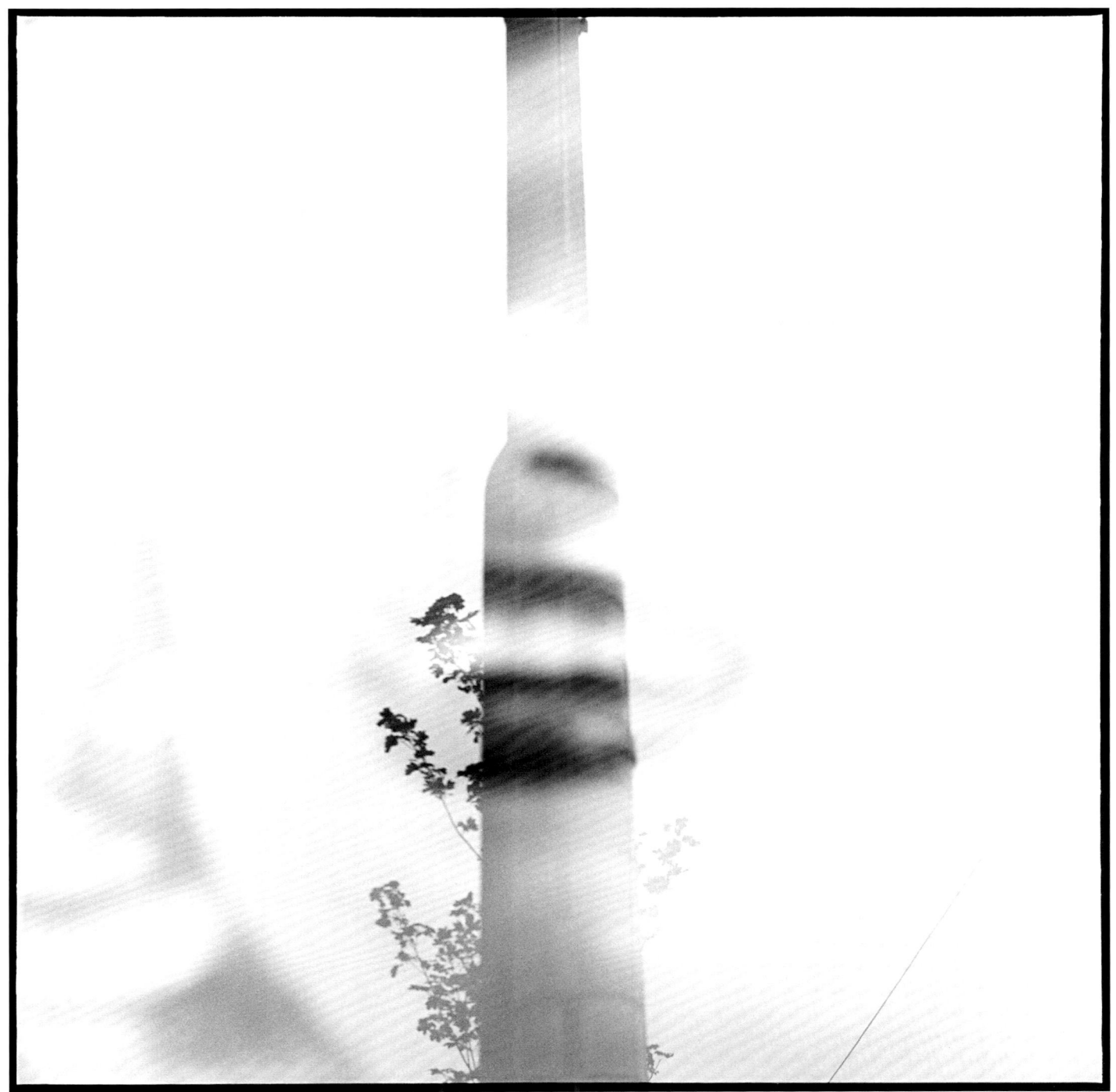

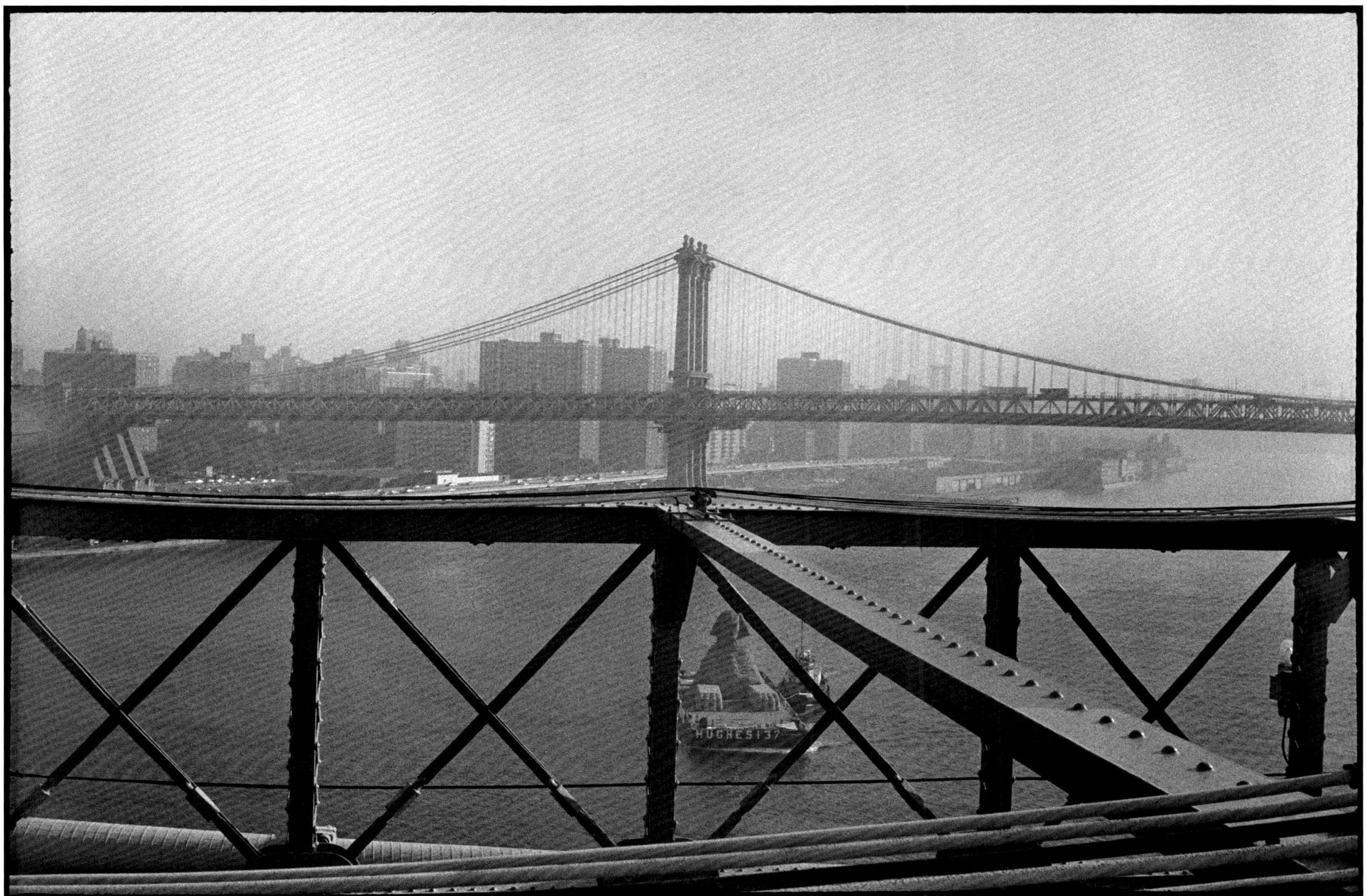

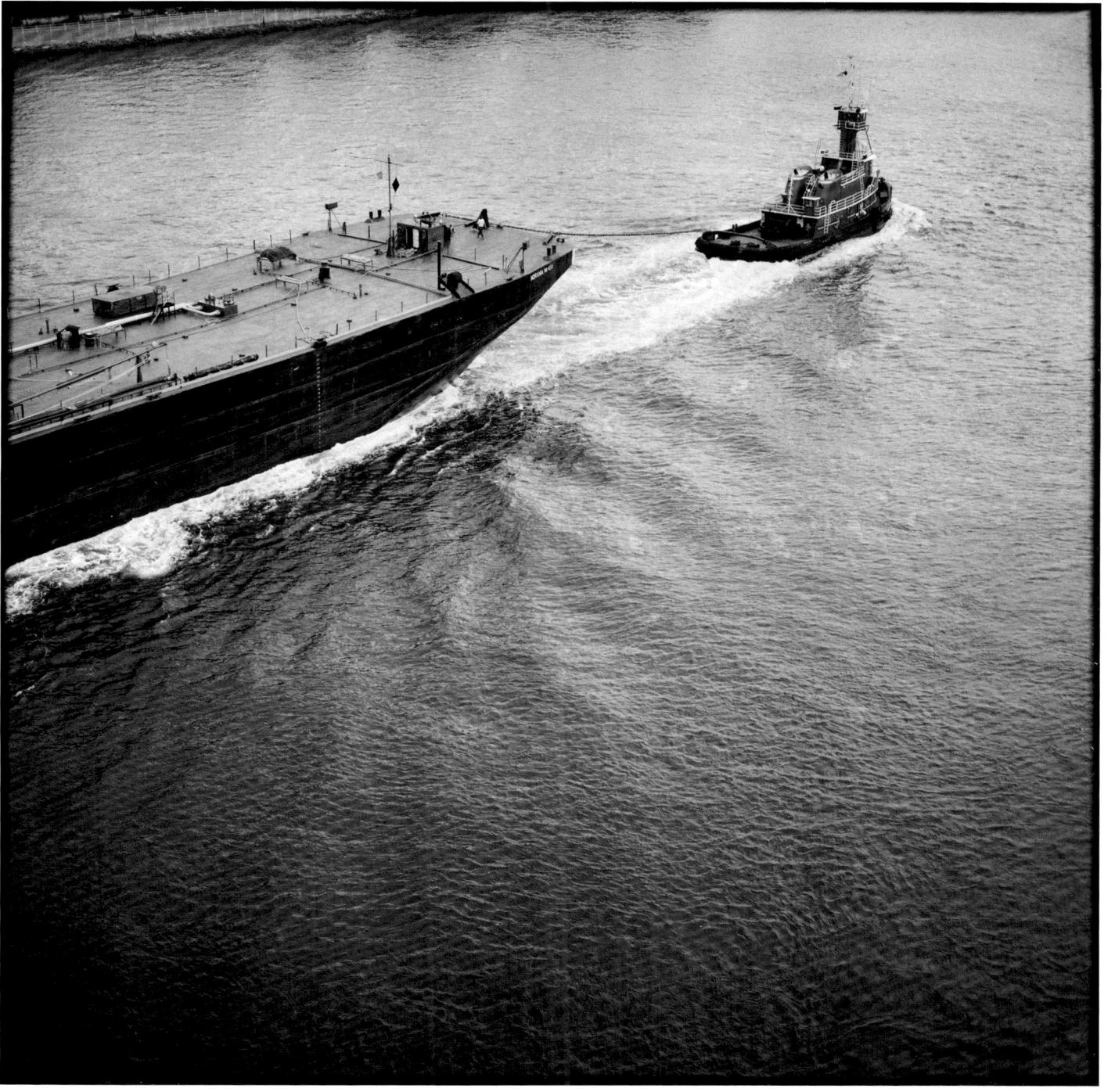

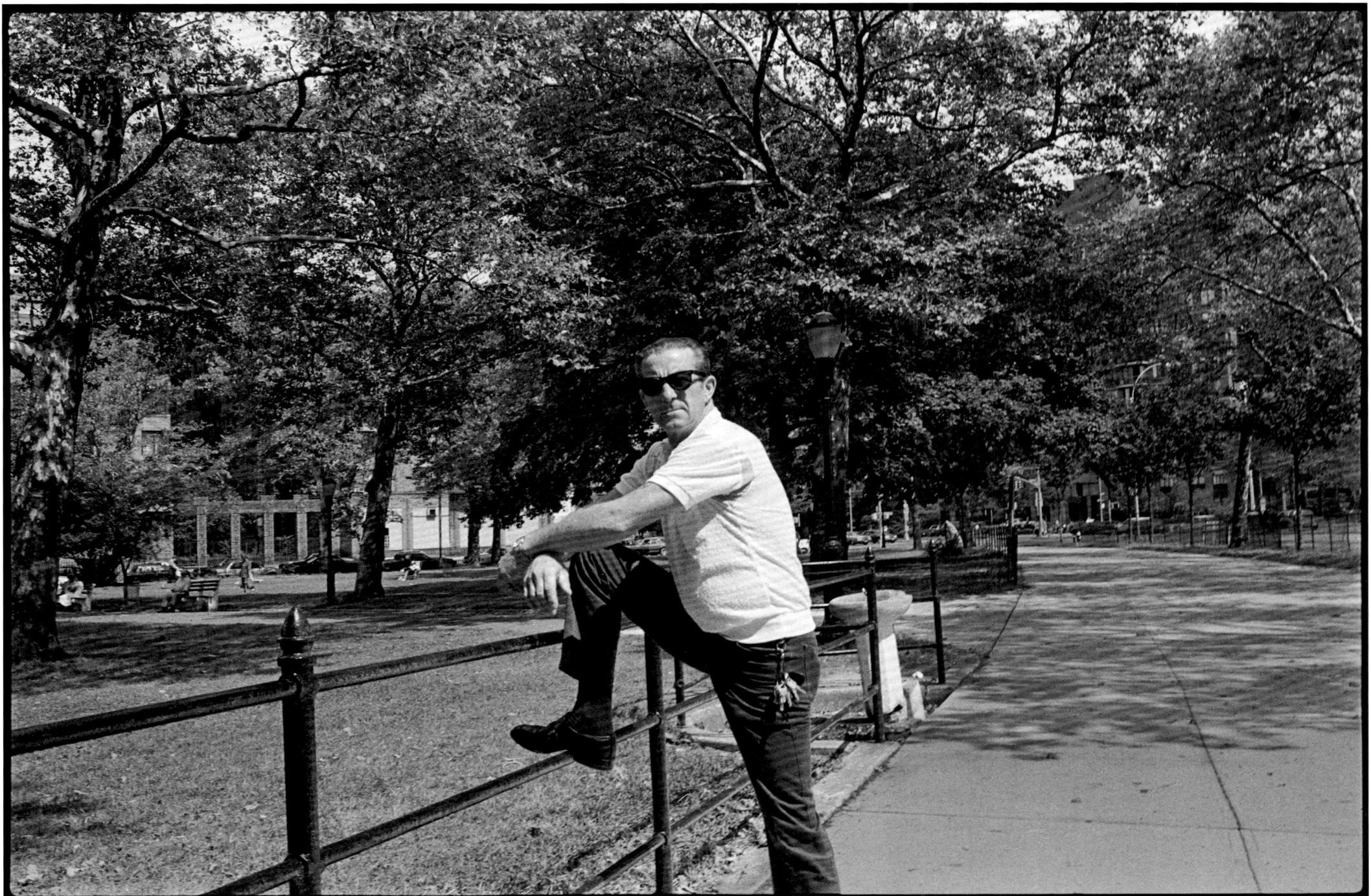

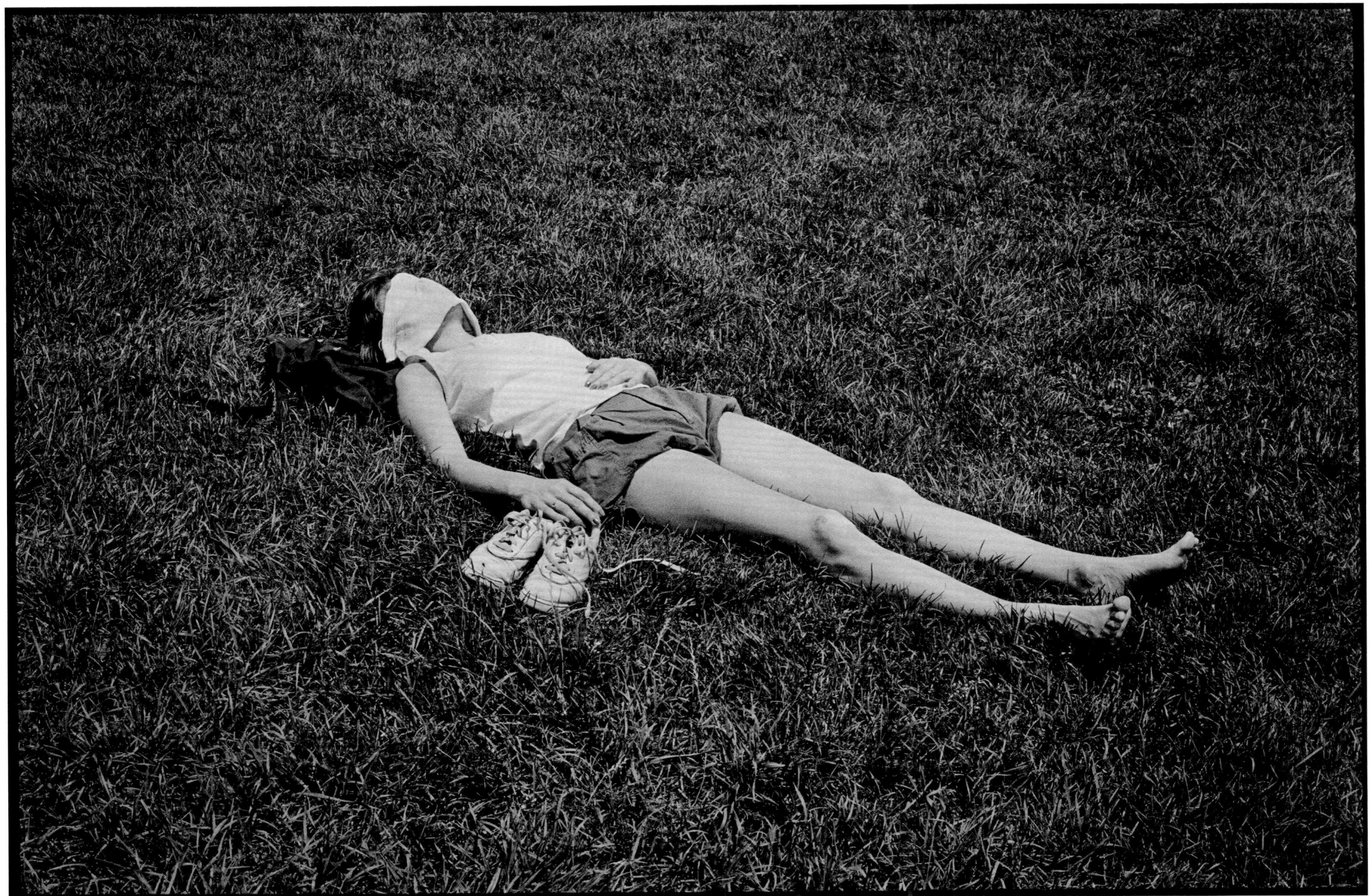

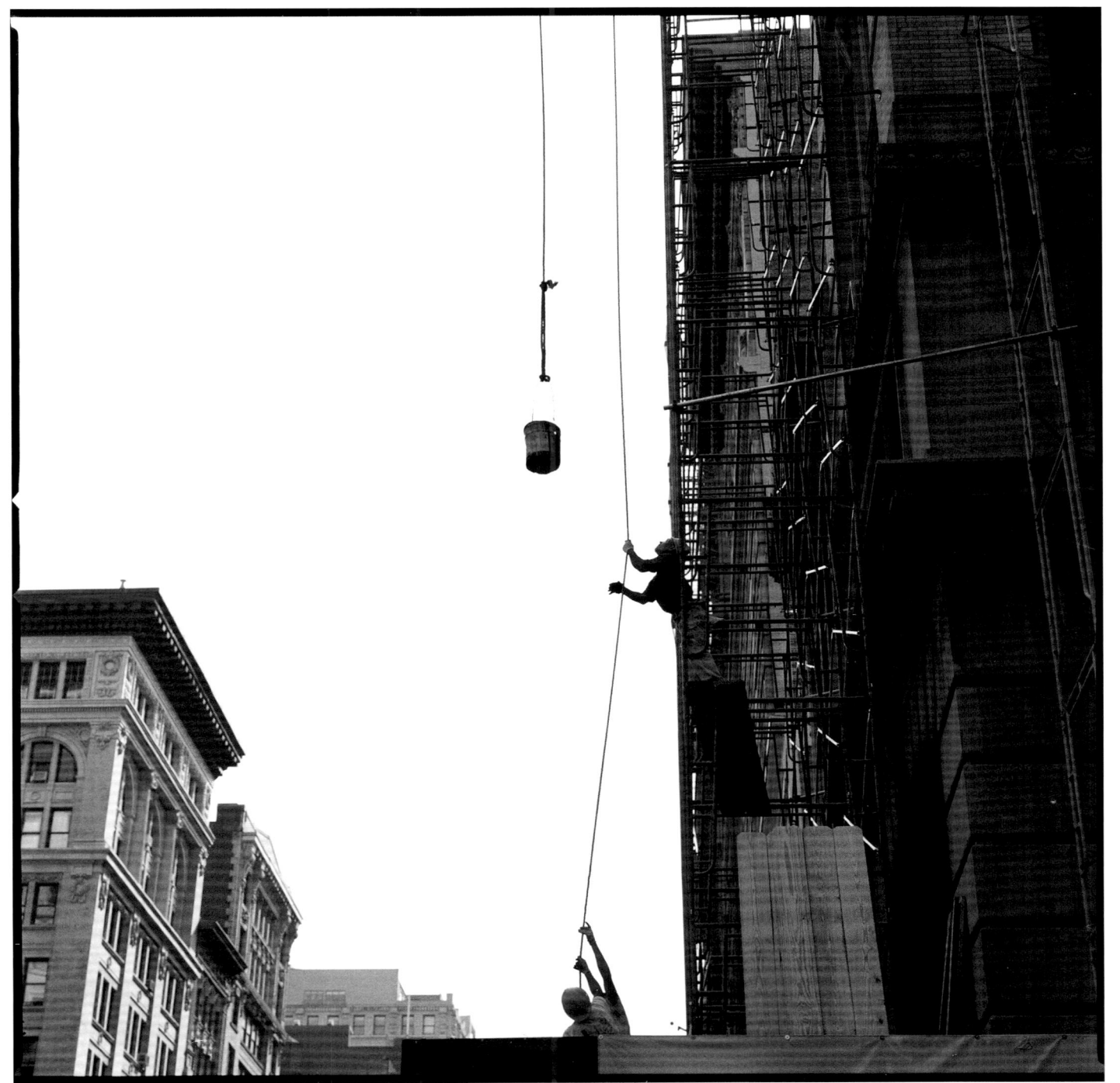

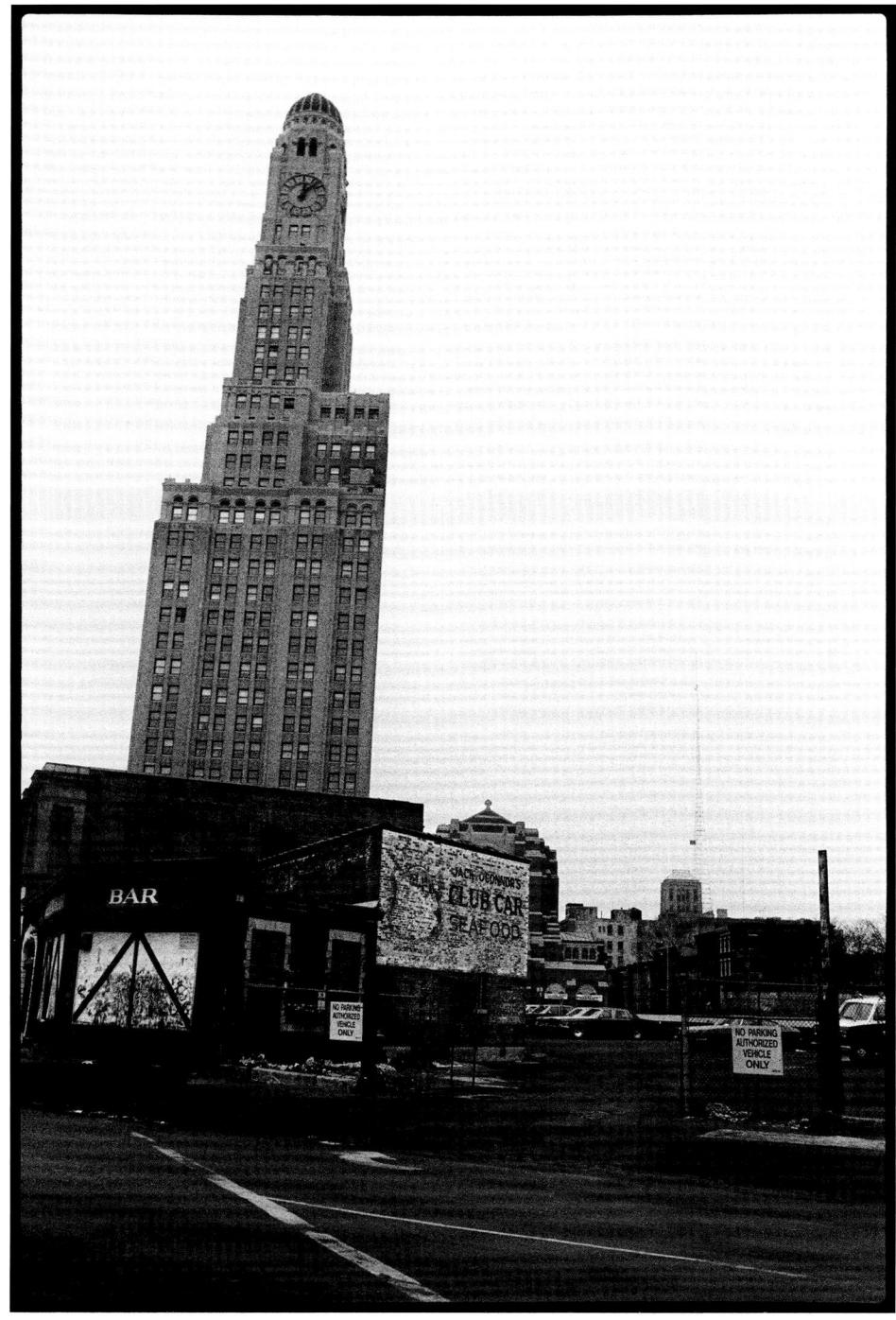

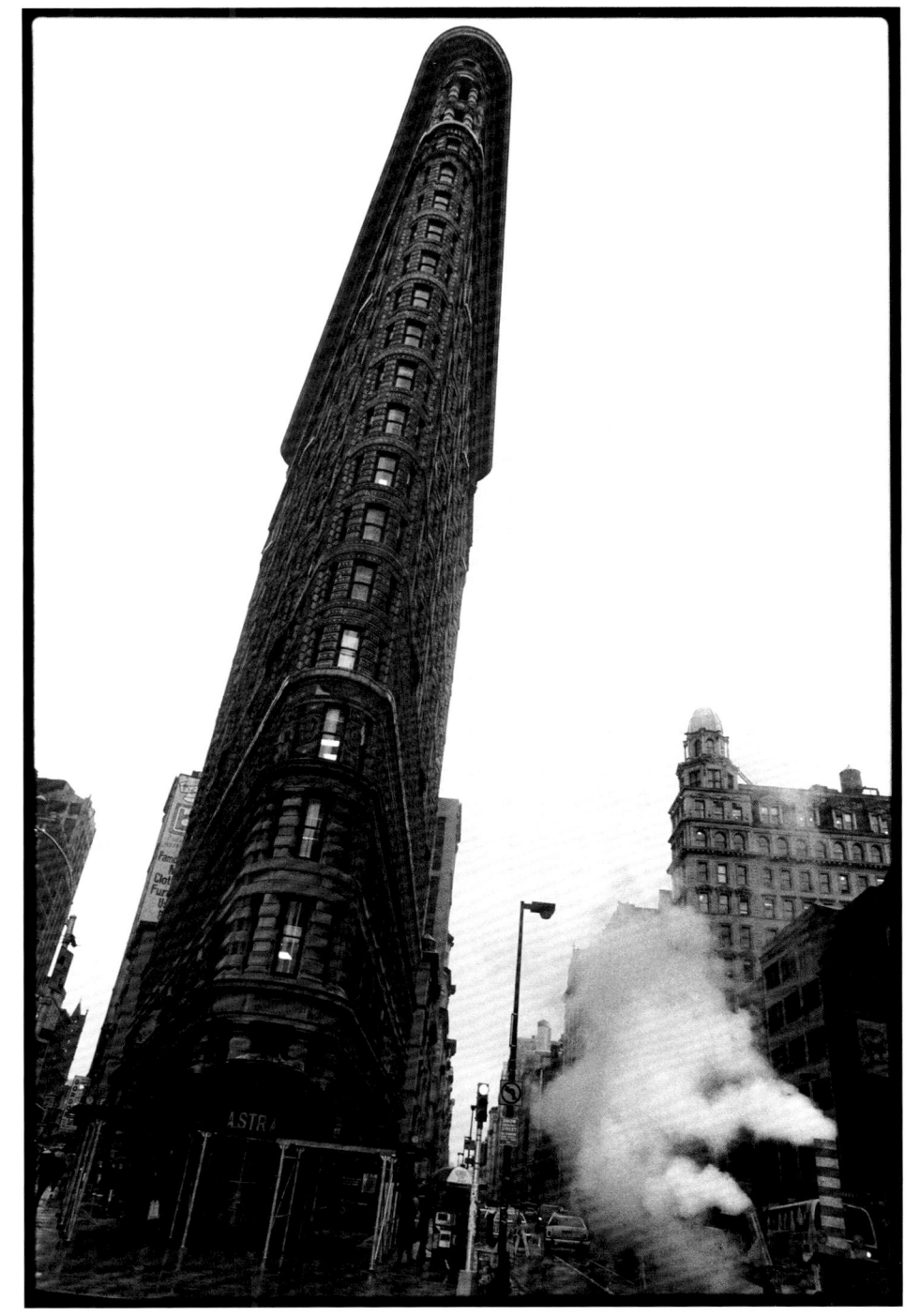

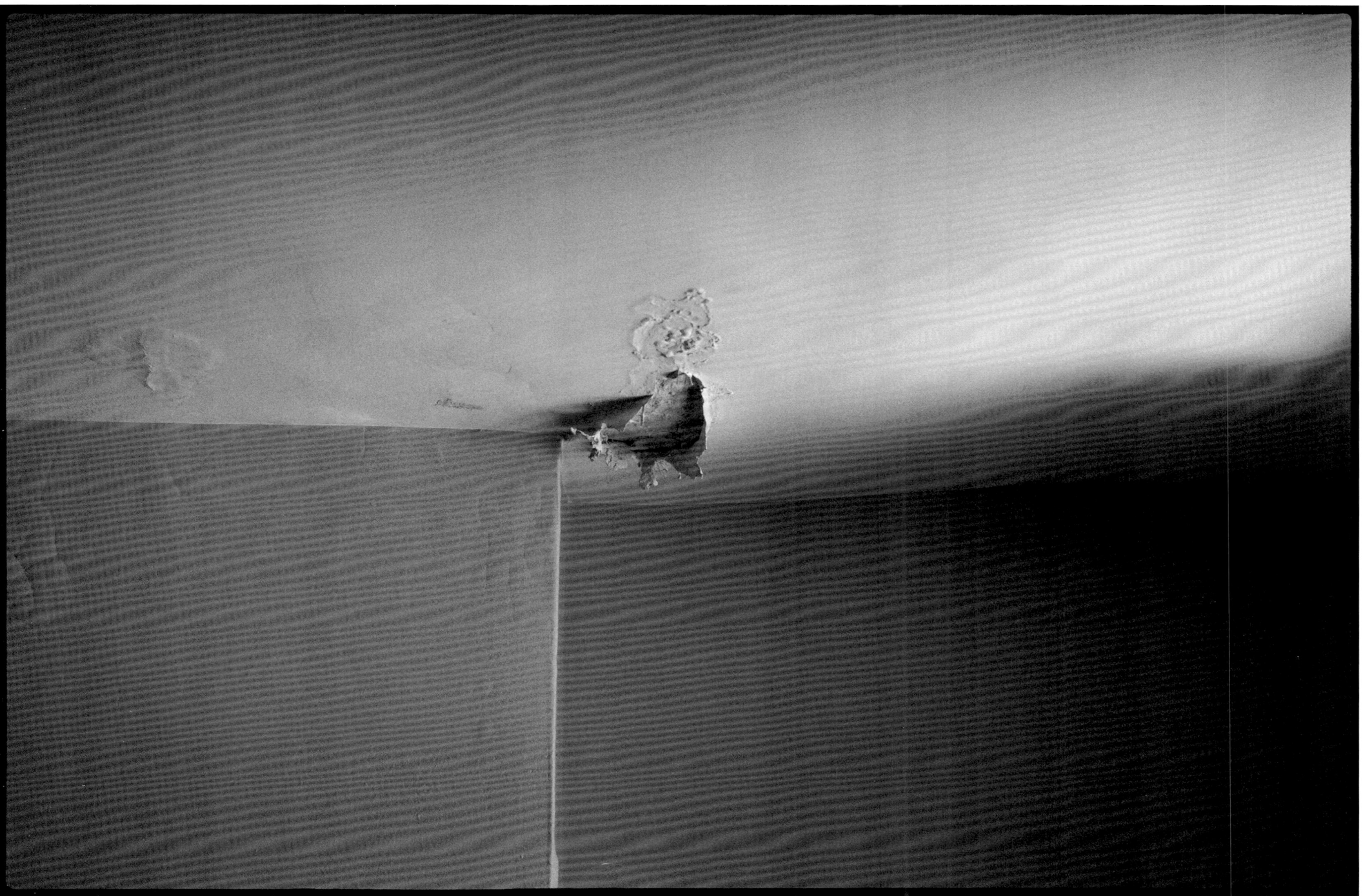

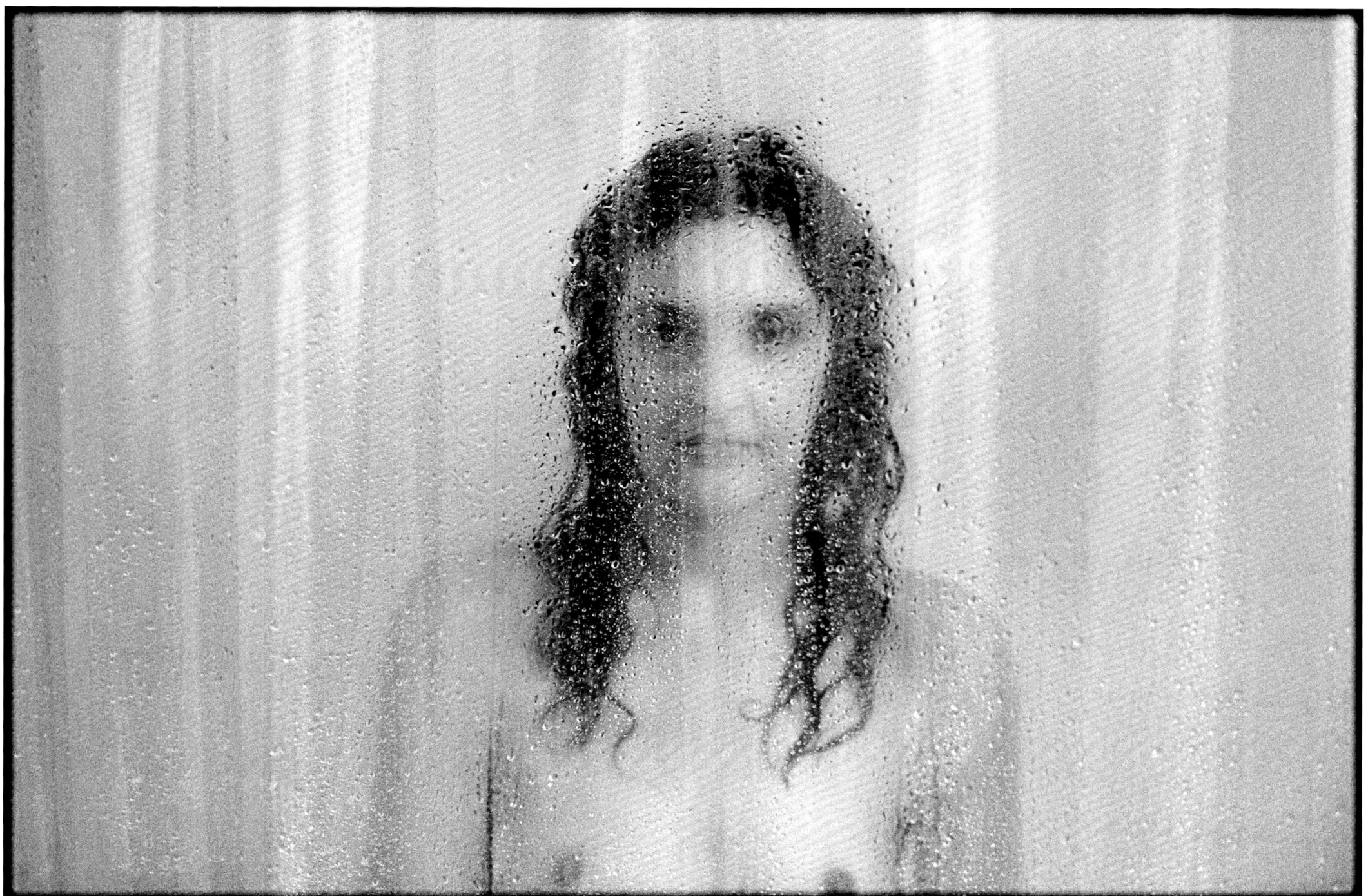

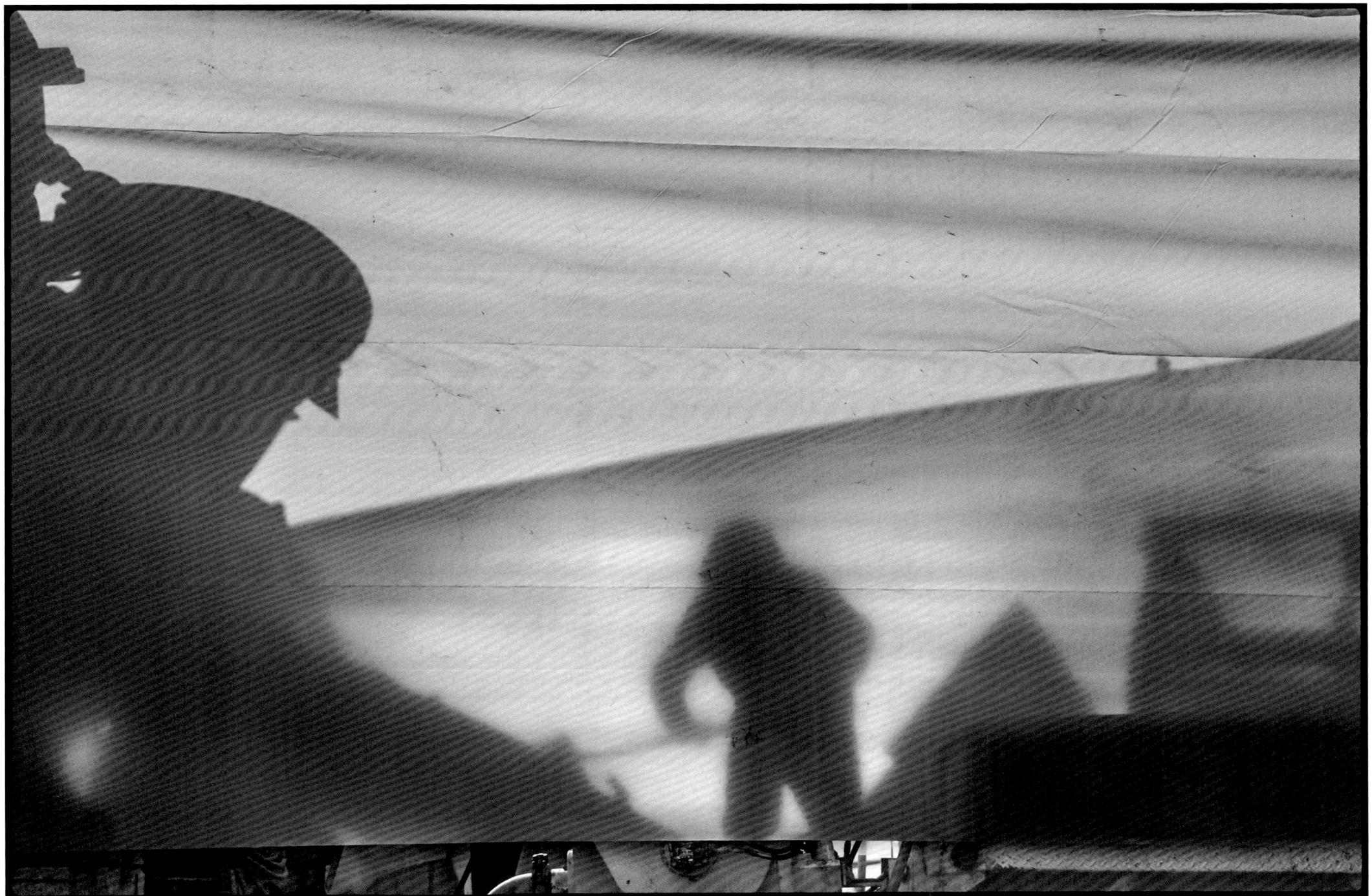

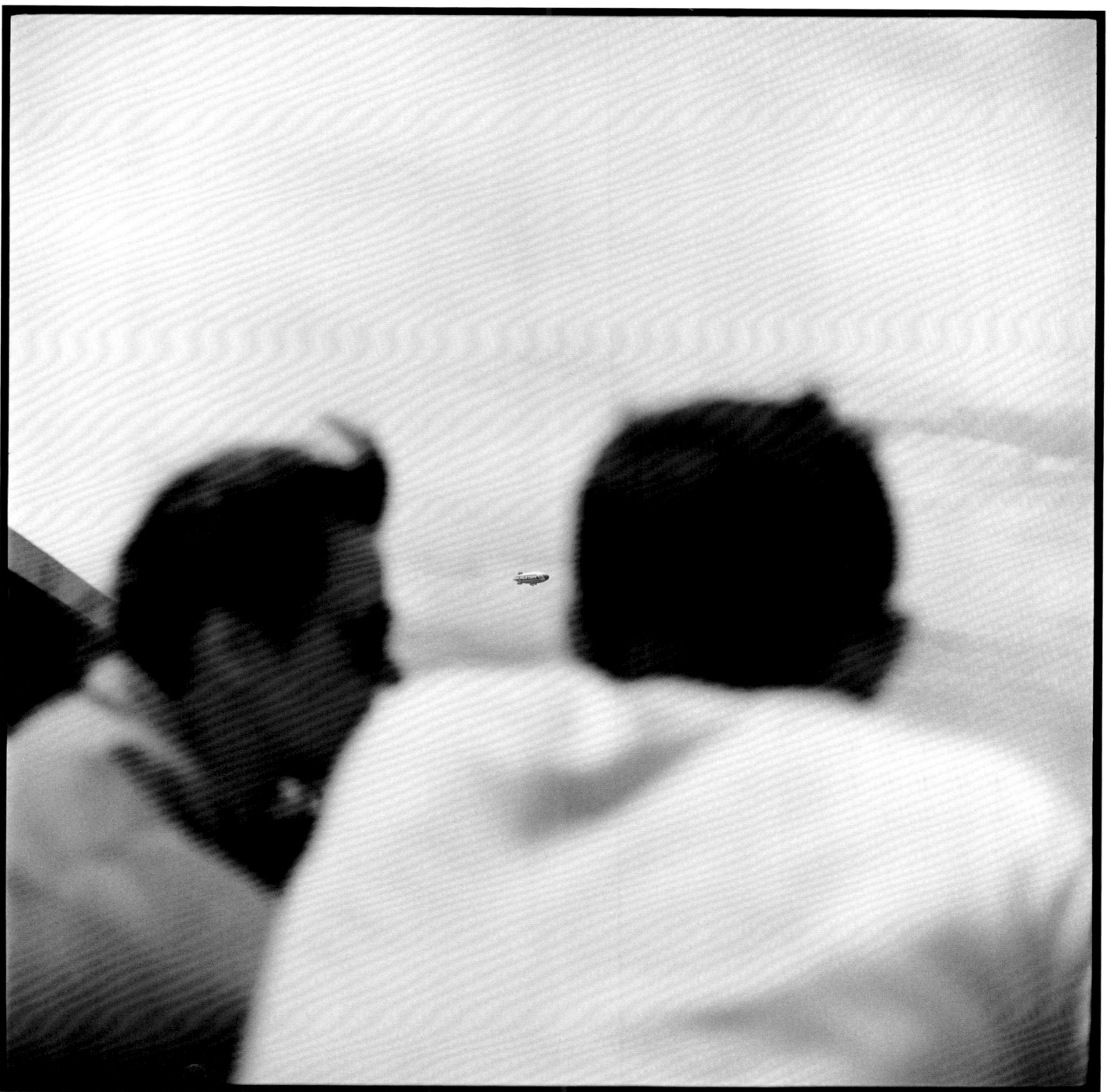

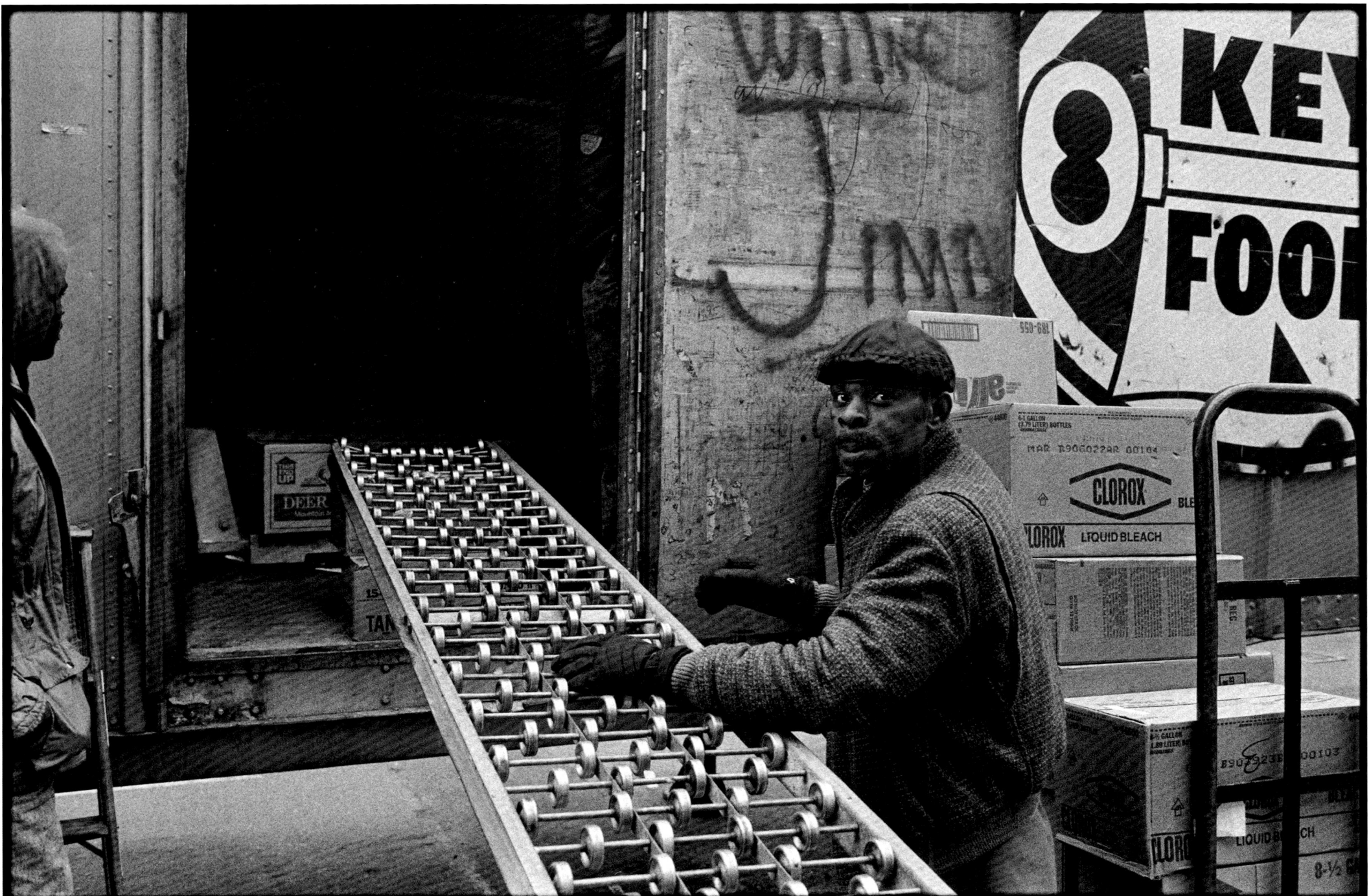

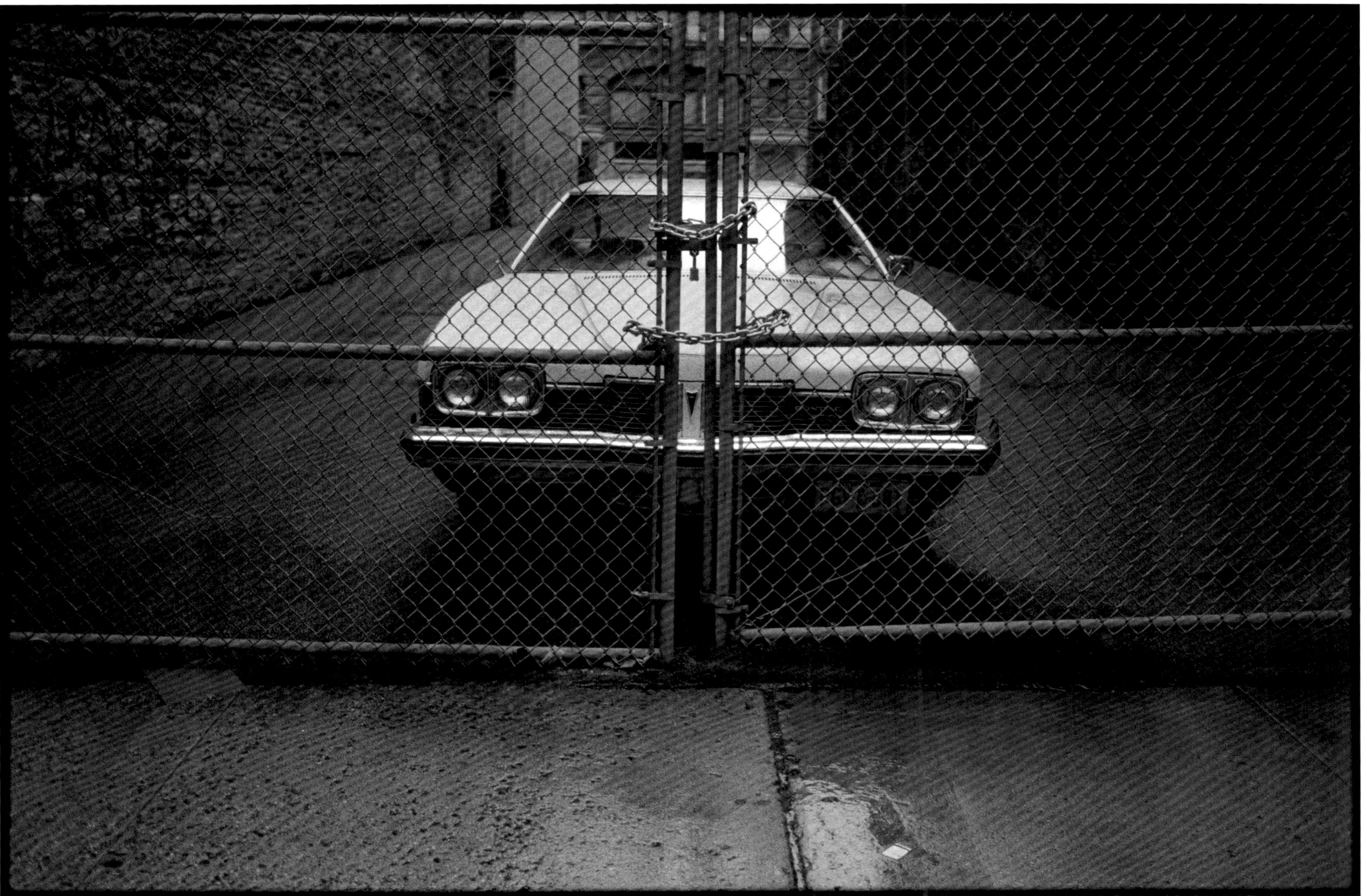

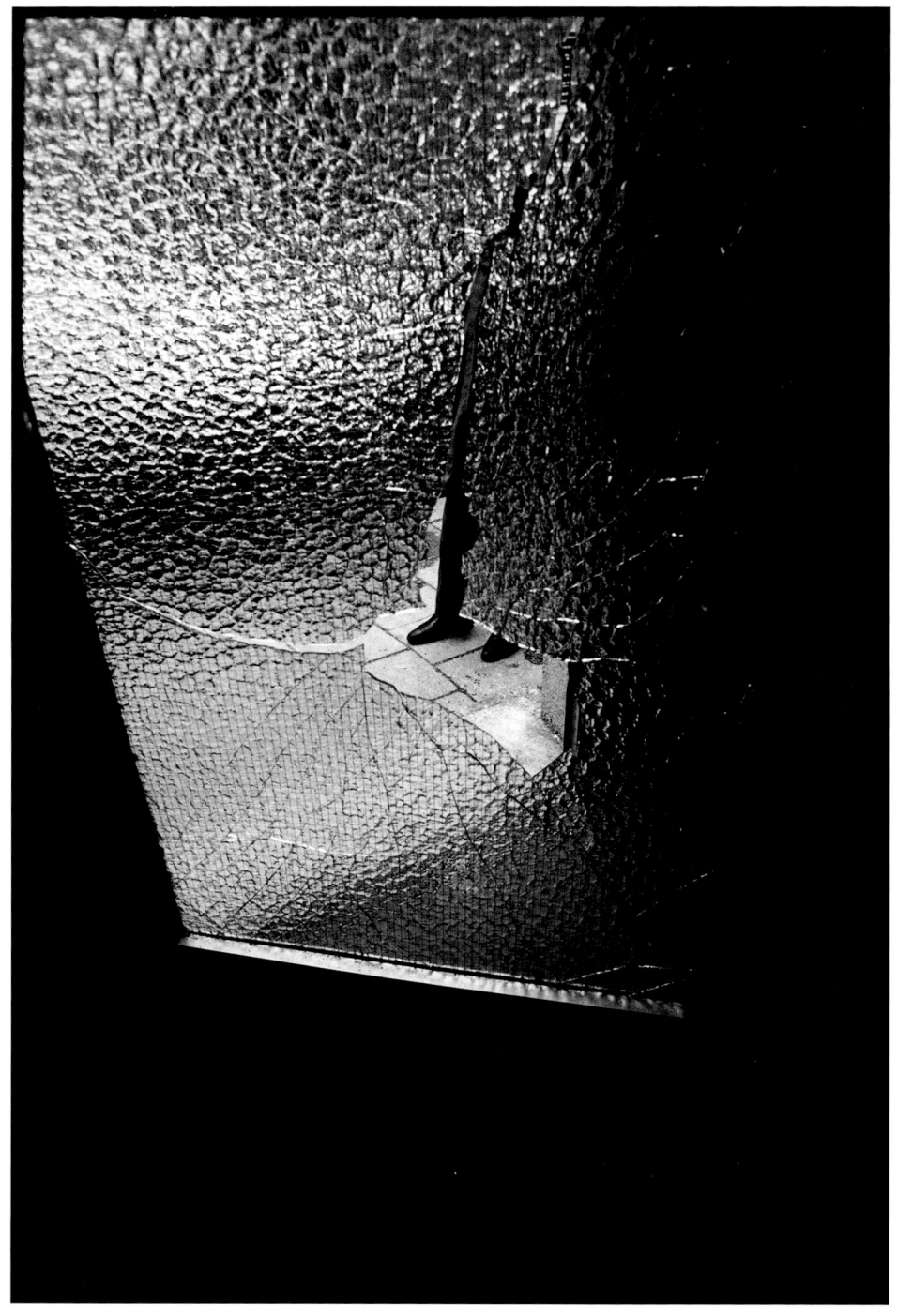

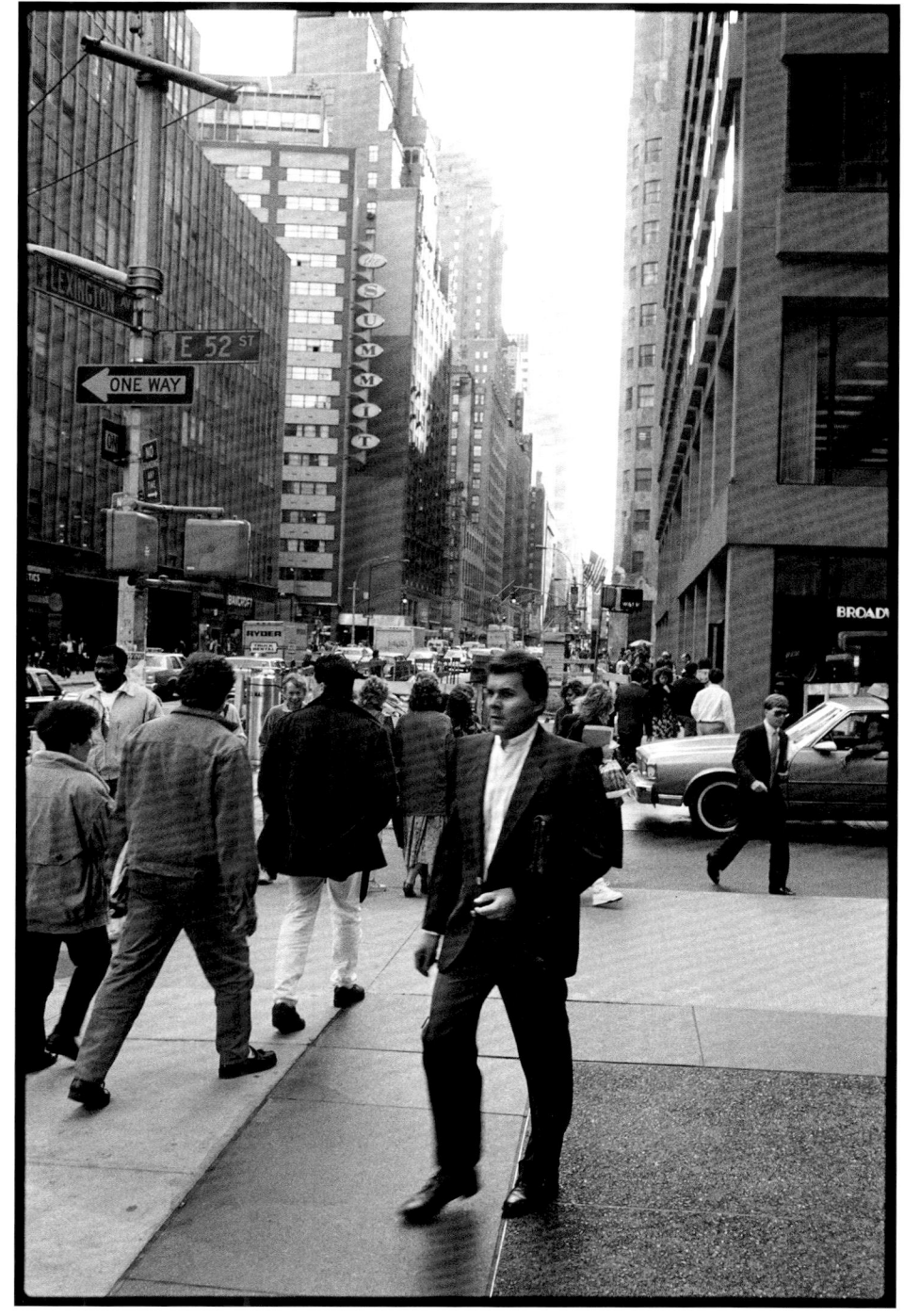

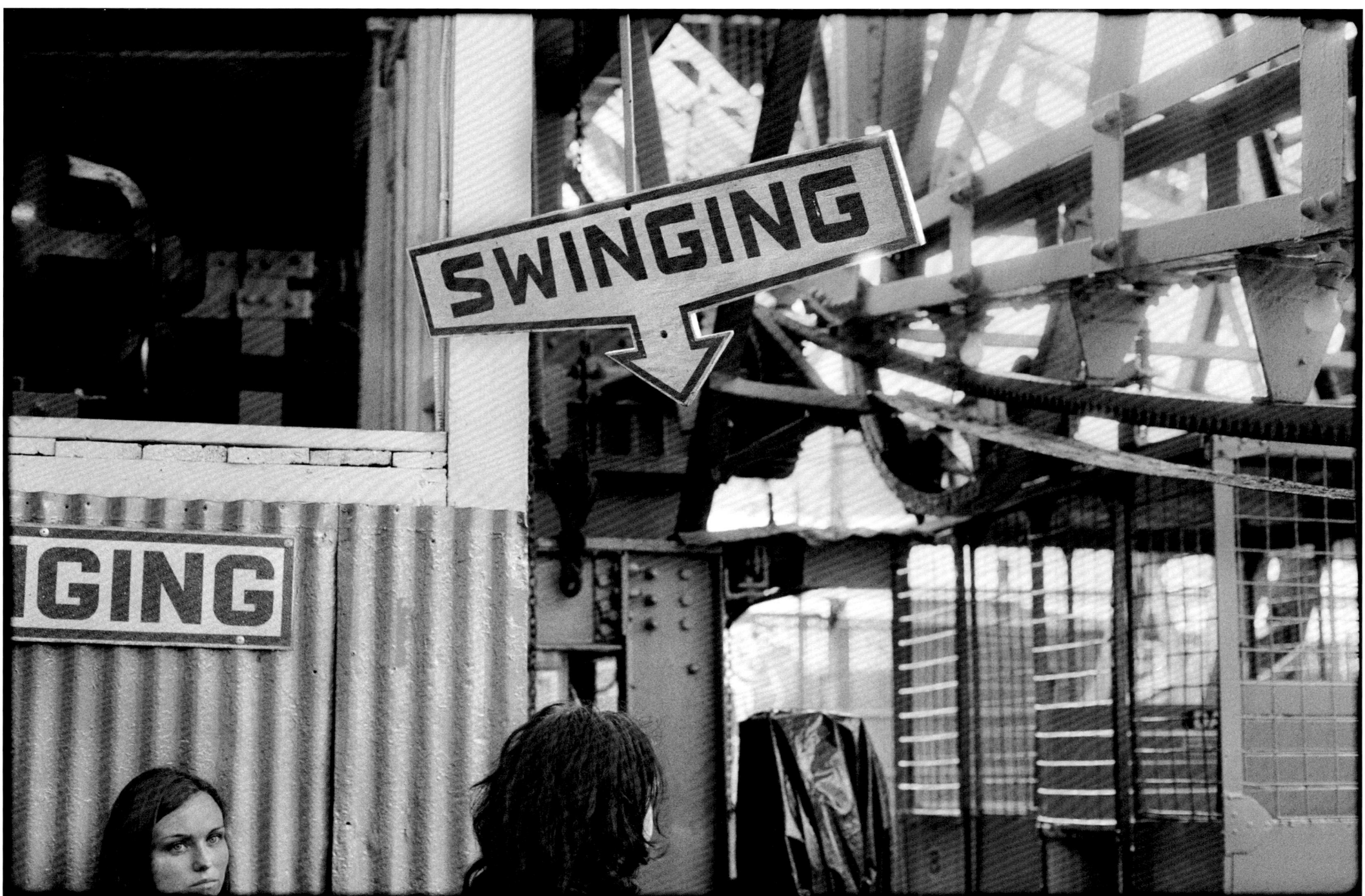

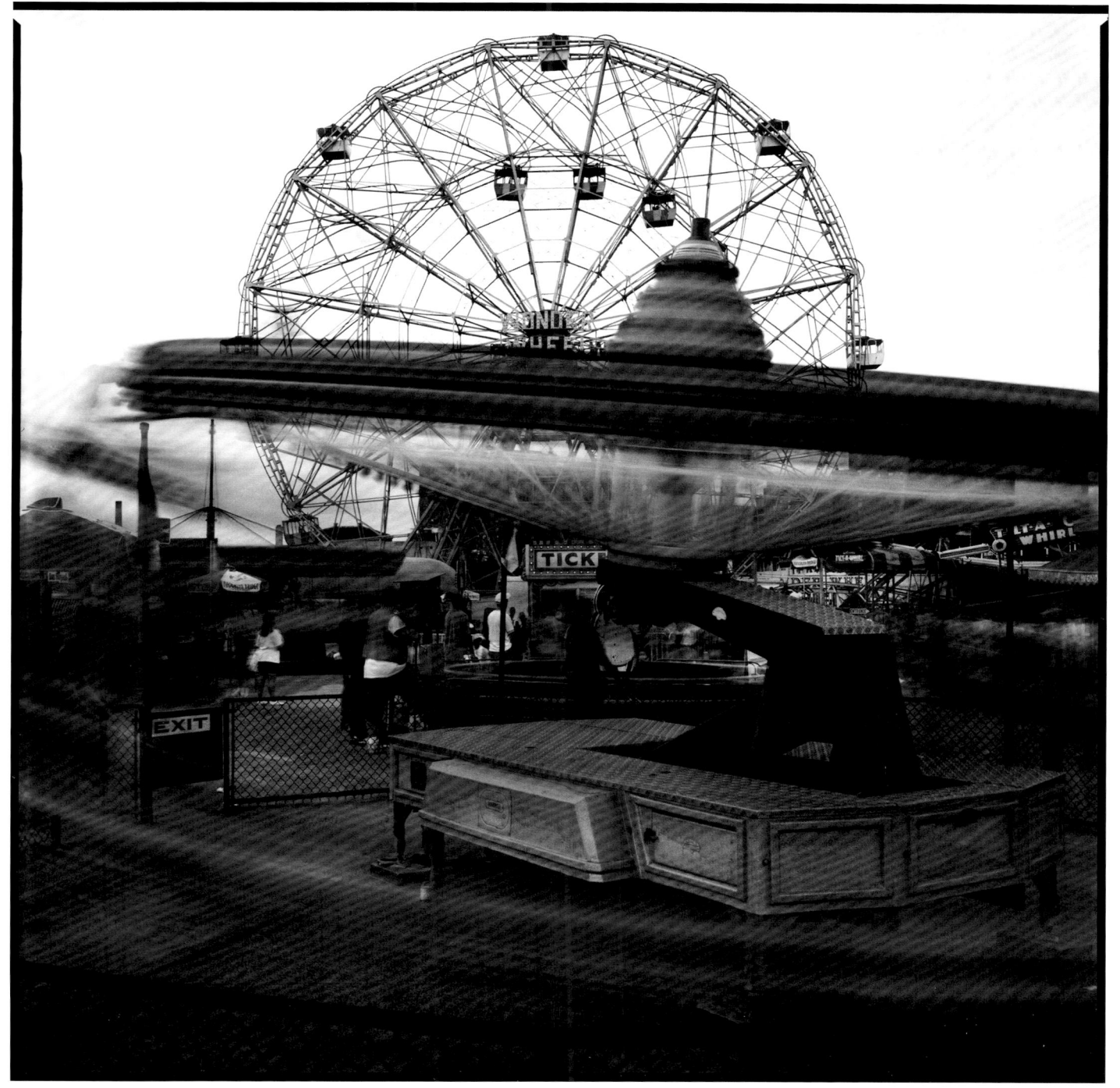

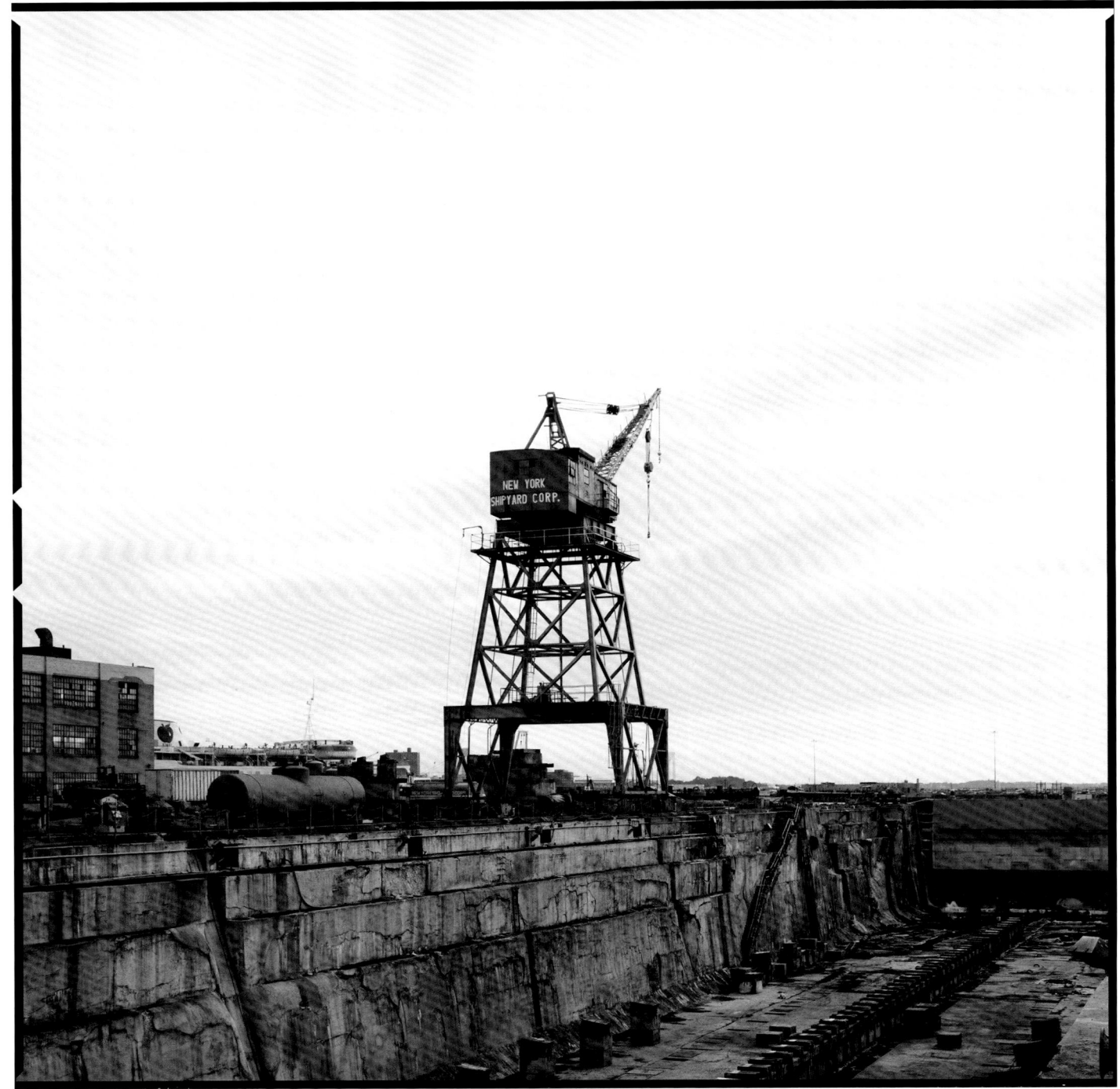

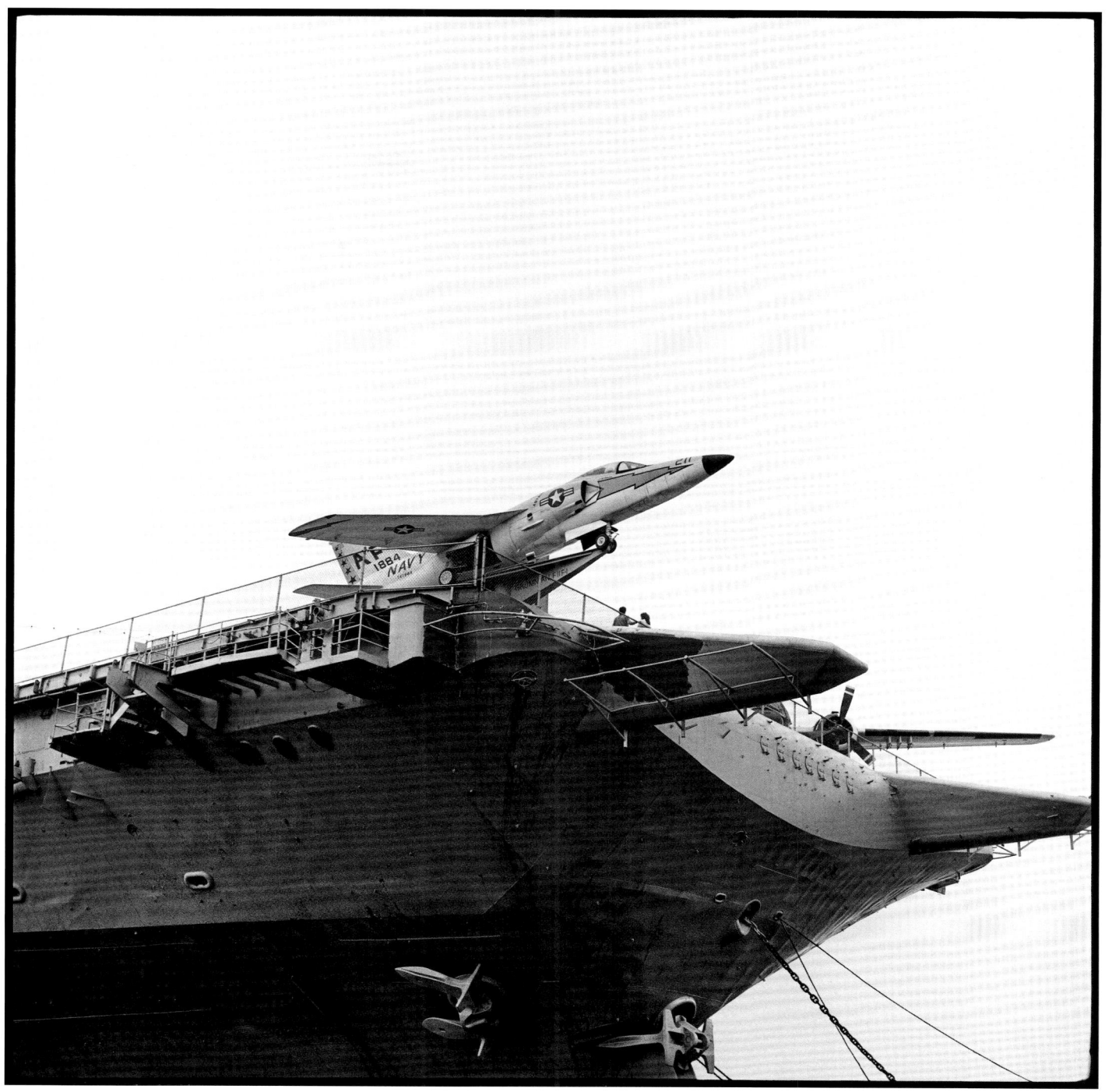

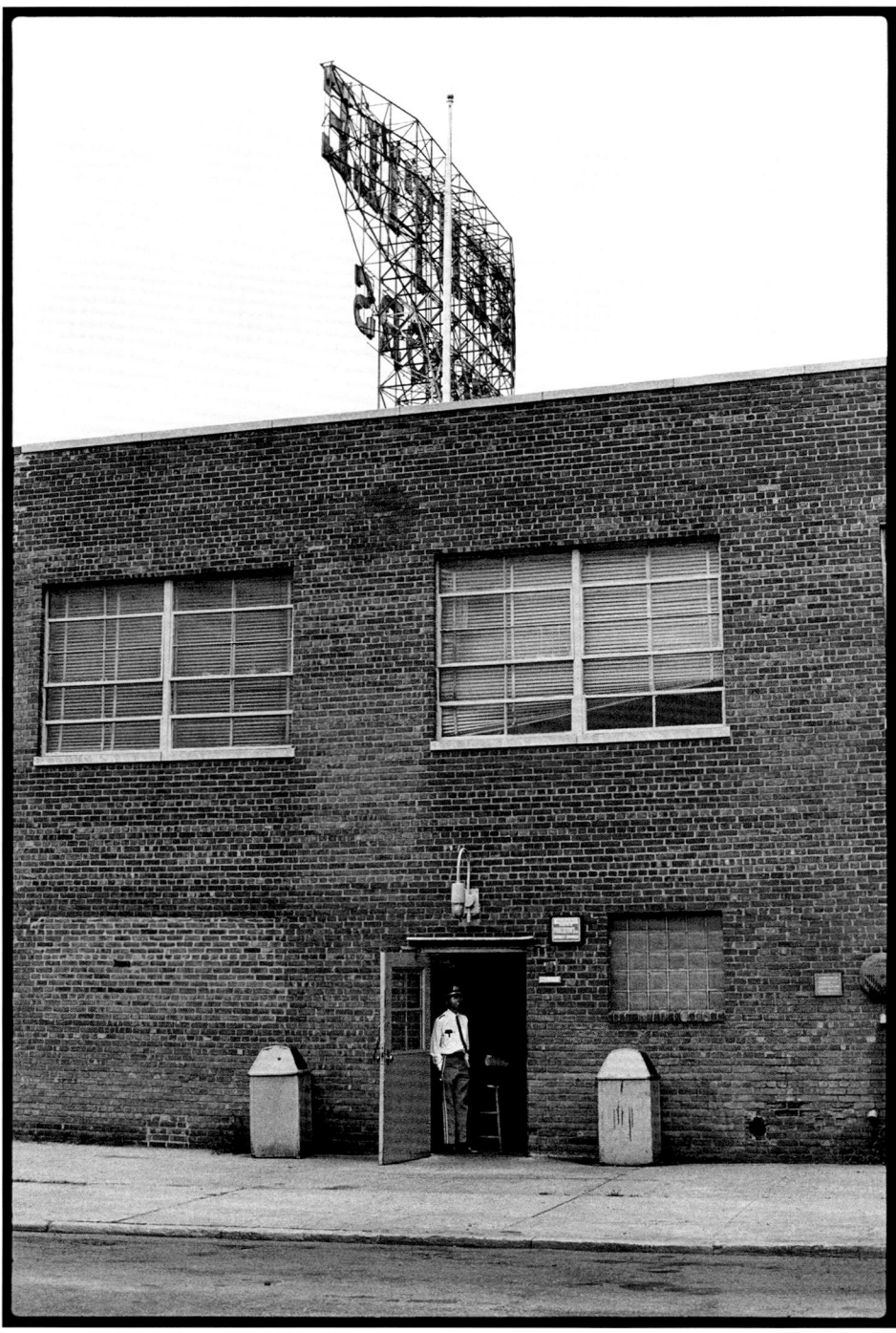

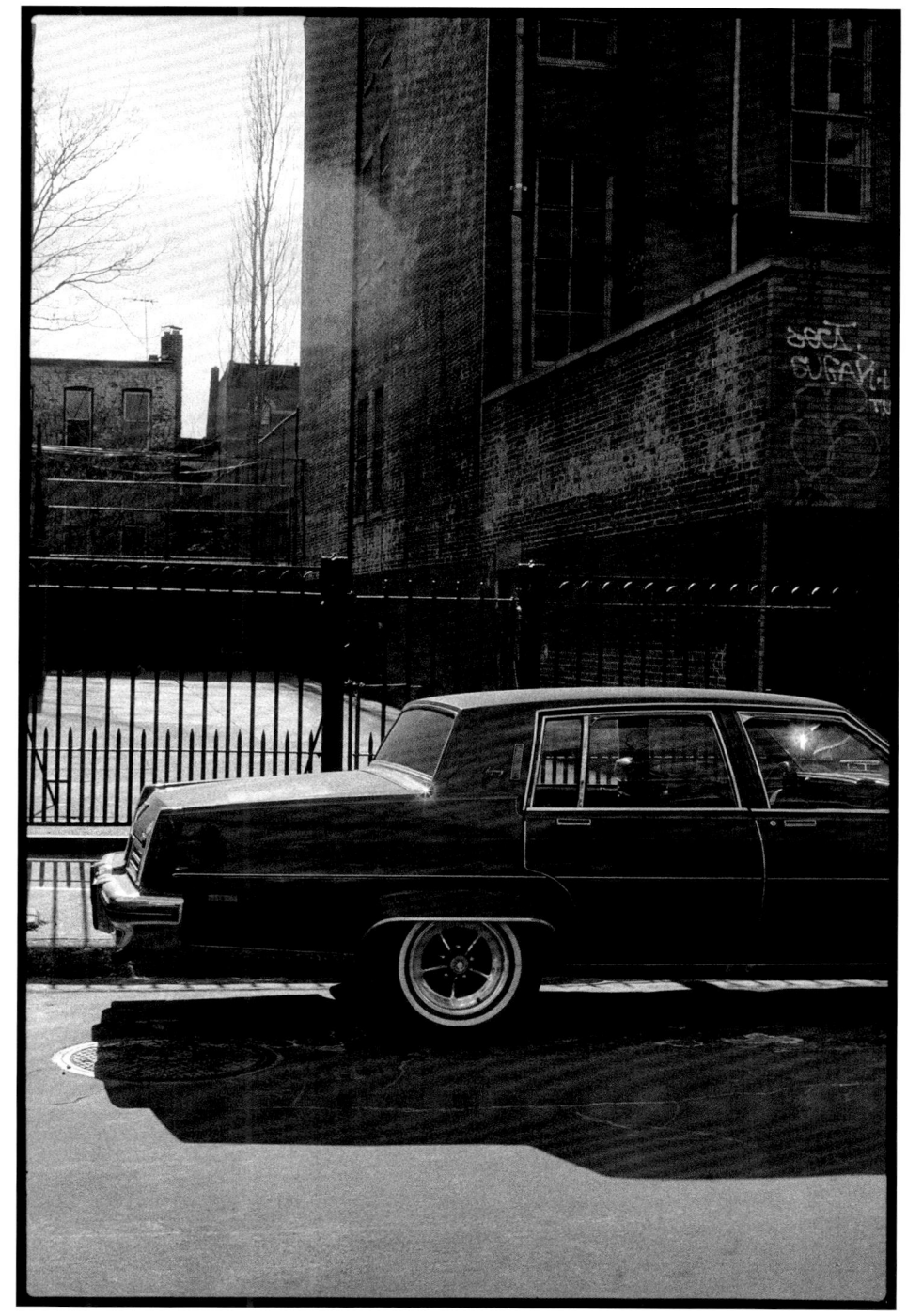

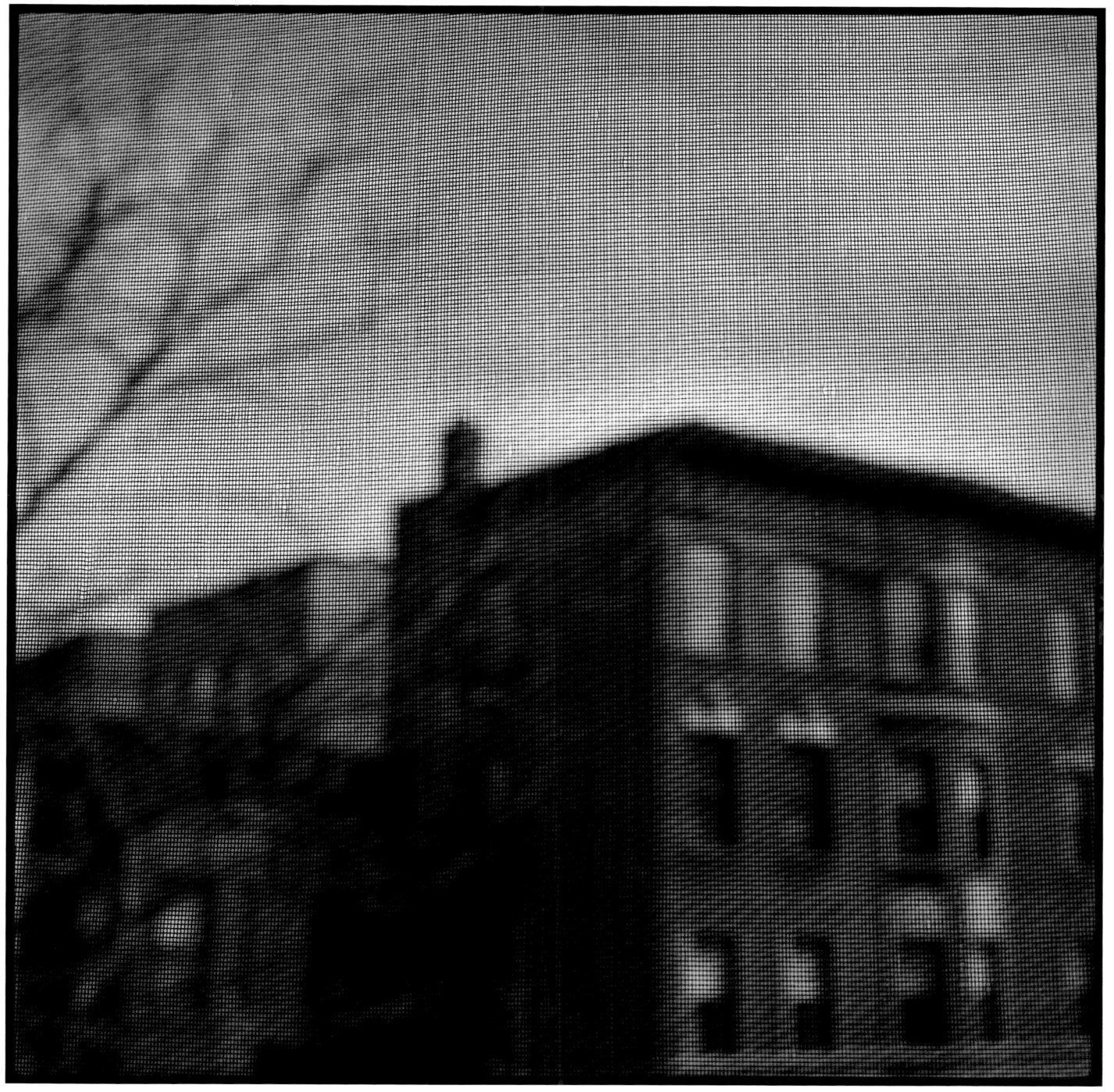

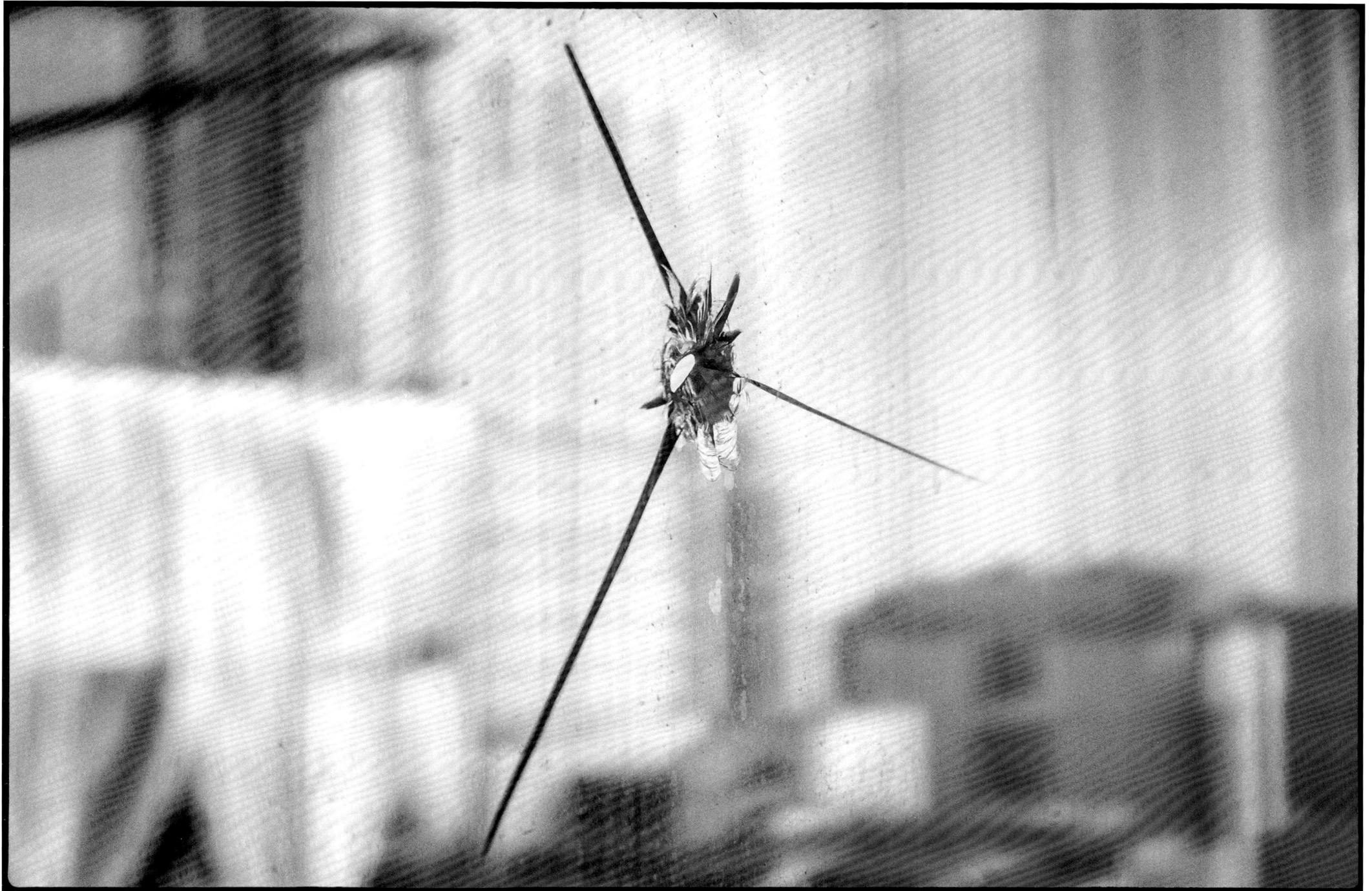

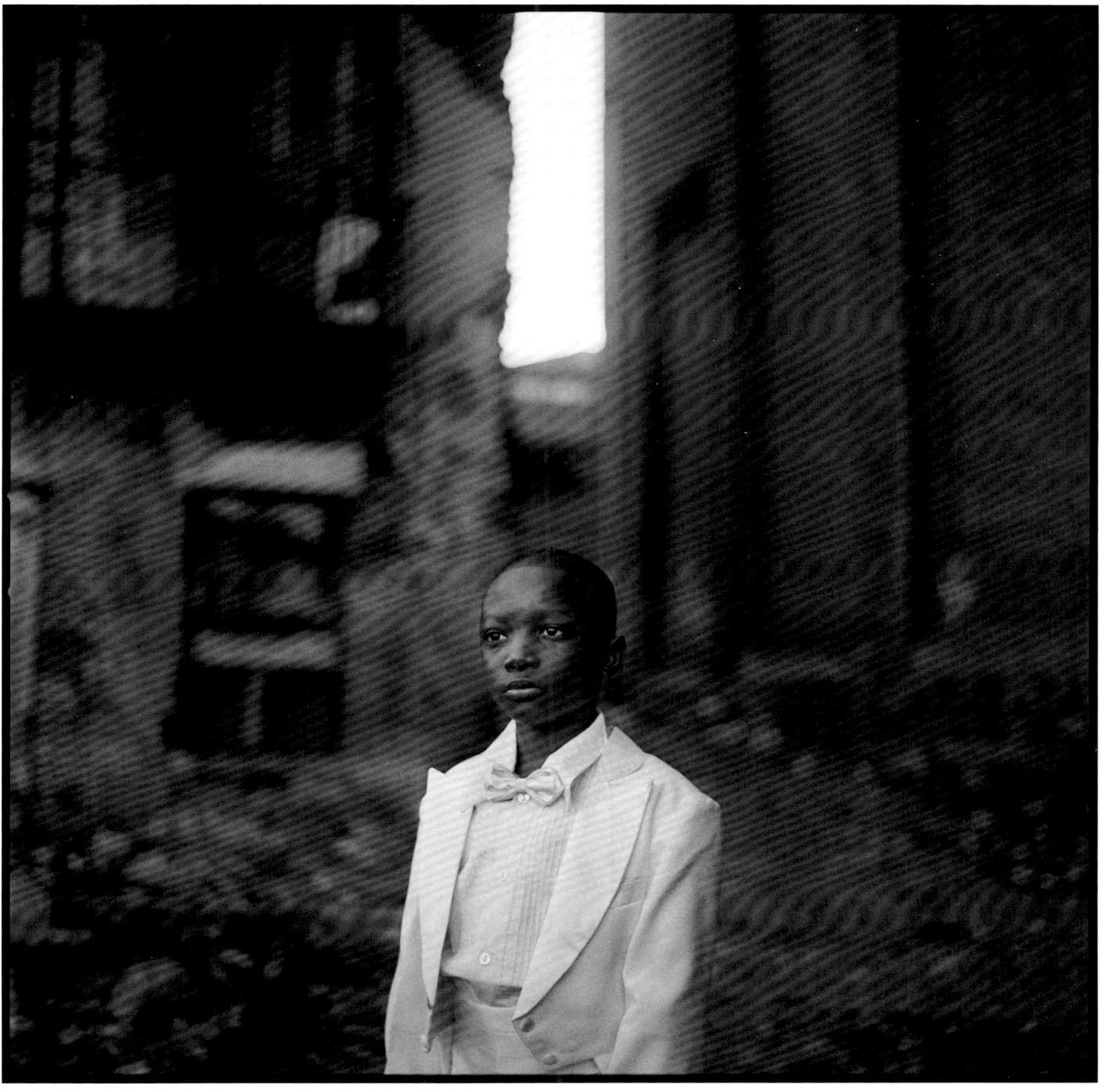

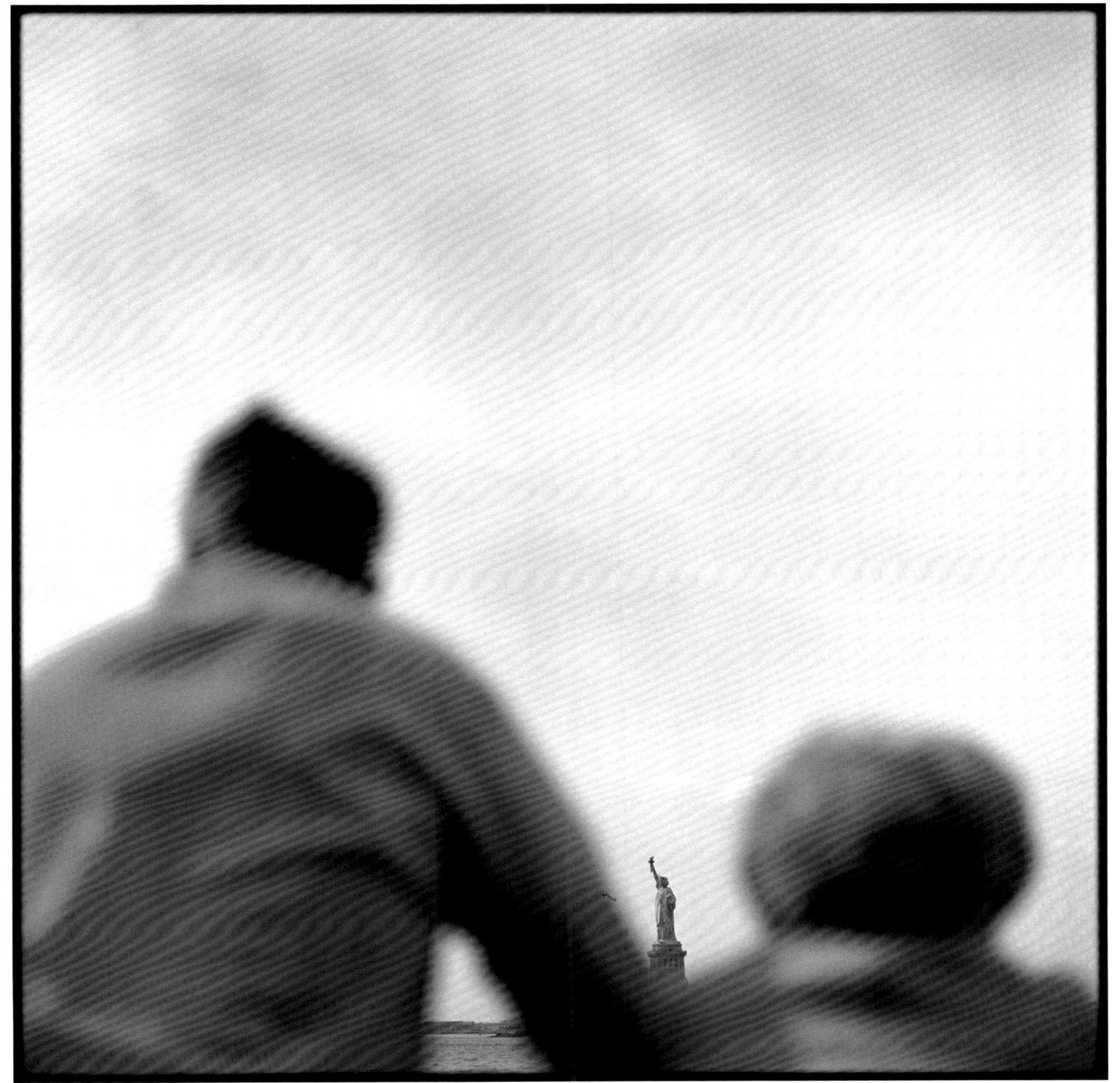

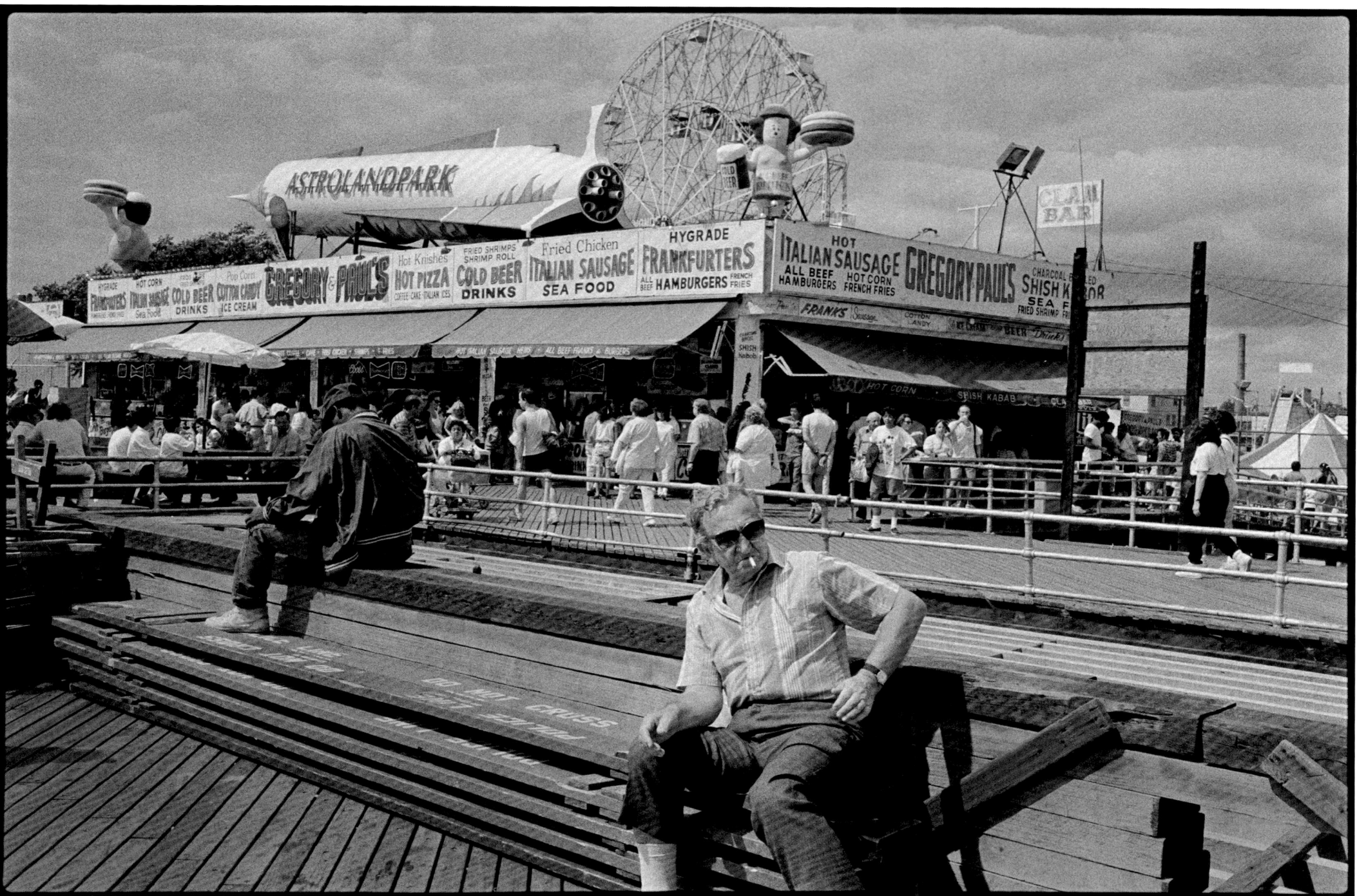

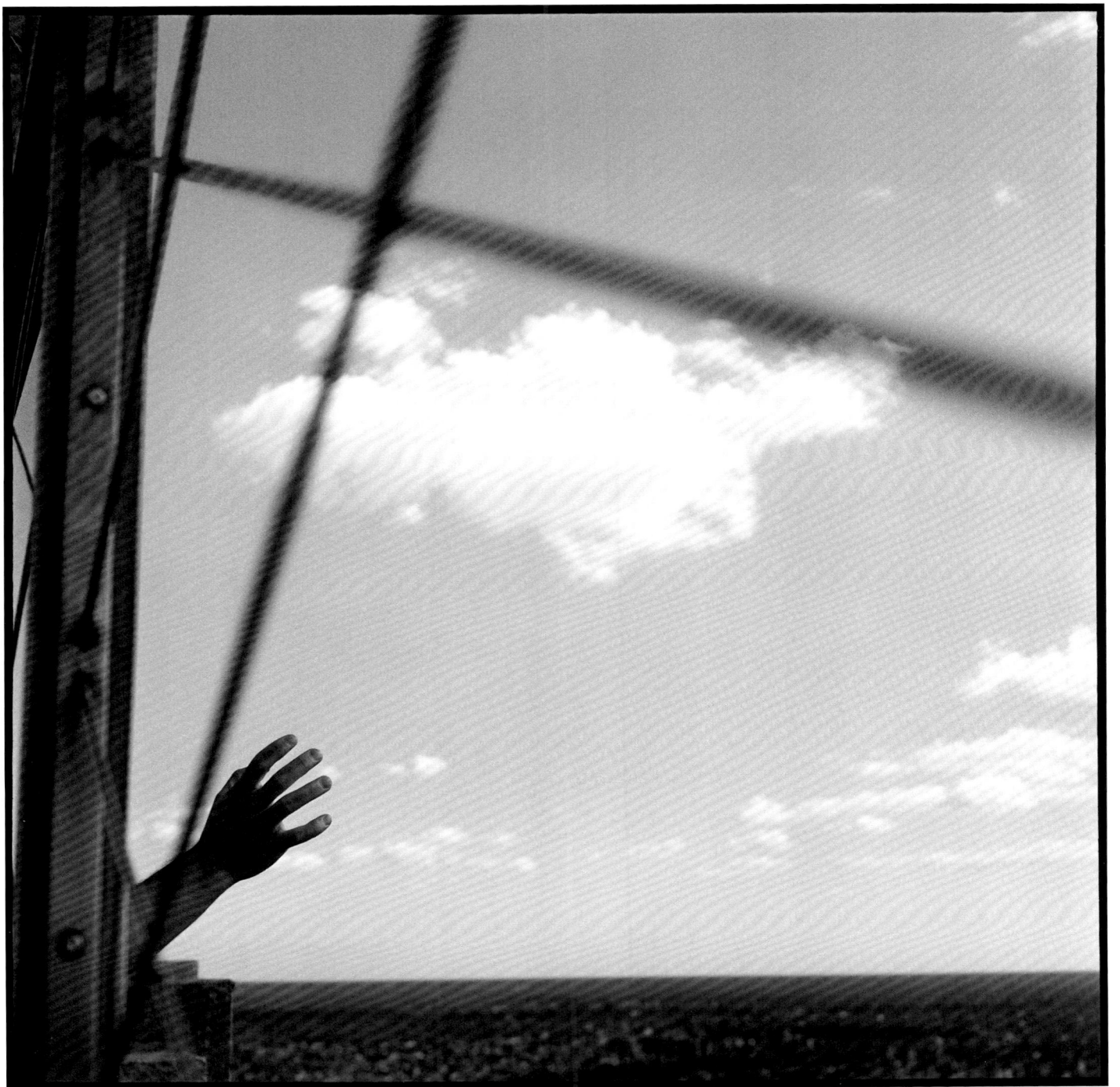

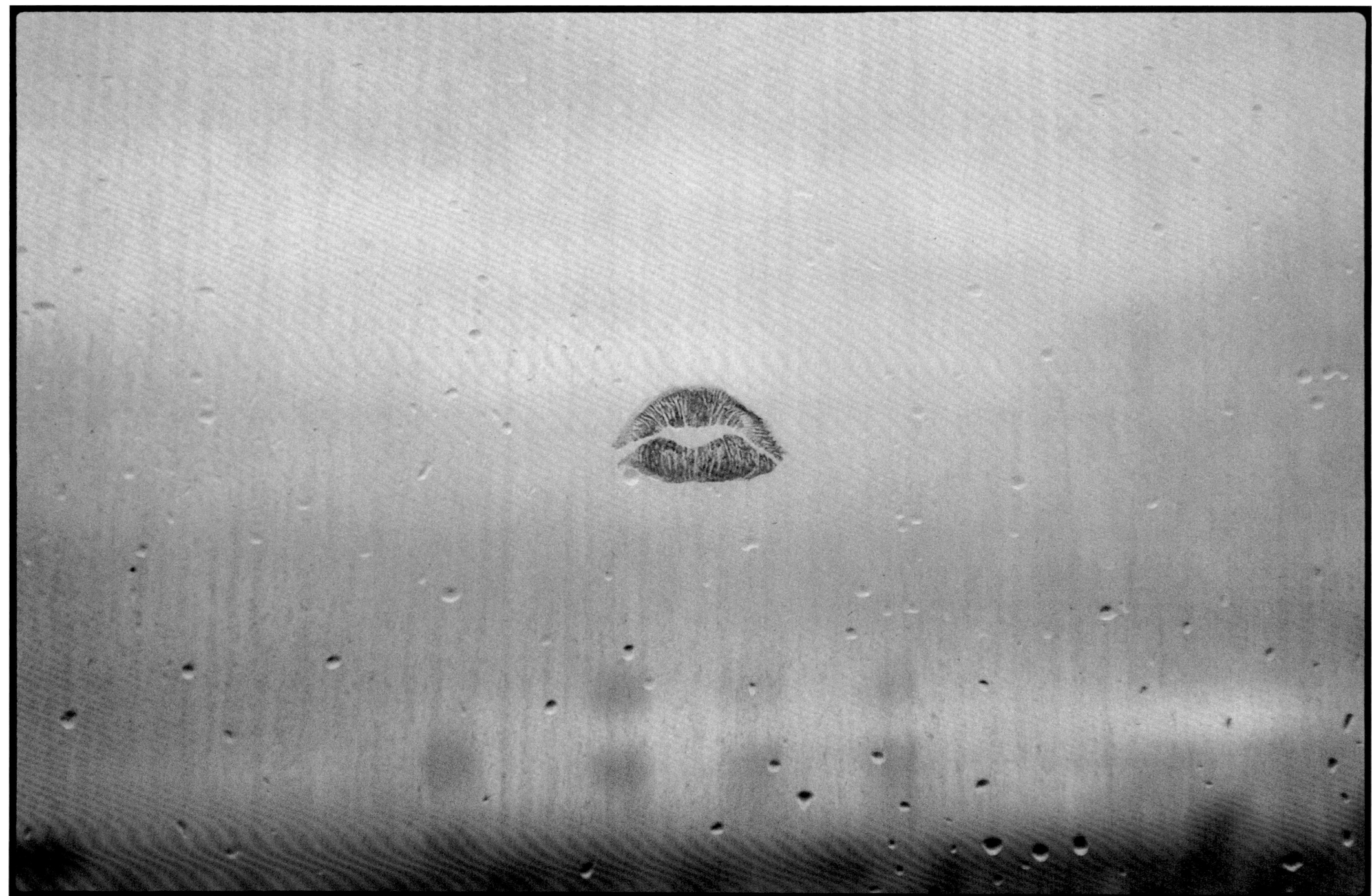

THE GREY GHOST It is a city unlike any I have known. One in which the sidewalks are a great equalizer and both kings and peasants share the pavement in a choreographed, democratic ballet. ¶ The sheer magnitude and seemingly infinite supply of energy in this great metropolis is incomprehensible. Upon first arrival, I was simultaneously paralyzed and inspired, provoked into a state of fear and wonderment. ¶ The myriad smells, hot flashes, chaos, and drone of car horns overcame me. This grand symphony occurs with such frequency and persistence, it eventually becomes a shrill and continuous presence. You can count yourself a true denizen of the city only when these ever-present elements go unnoticed. ¶ As time passed I became a fragment of the organism, as vital a piece that any one person can occupy. The metamorphosis was underway and my deep love for one of the world's most spirited and influential of places began to blossom. ¶ I was a transplant and a true novice to the fanfare that surrounded me at every turn. ¶ It was the moment that must occur in every serious artist's life, where amid the fury I struggled to find my voice, that elusive method that informs the manner in which we perceive and interpret our surroundings. ¶ I'm a traditionalist at heart and I have a deep love of the longstanding practice of photographing in public spaces. In 1987 I was courted and seduced by New York. She took me in and showed me the vulnerability that lies beneath her hardened shell. ¶ Throughout the history of the photographic medium, she has acted as a proving ground and a rite of passage for countless photographers. The list reads as a testament to this great place. Thankfully, many have roamed her streets and shared their journey with us. ¶ It was Alfred Stieglitz who, in the later part of the 19th century, all but invented the form. Stieglitz was among the first to realize and exploit the swiftness with which one was able to photograph in the streets with a hand-held camera. He created images within her that have come to define her. Paul Strand, a young protégé of Stieglitz, photographed her streets succinctly. Together, the collective vision of Stieglitz and Strand has stood as a benchmark in the discipline for more than a century. ¶ They were among the first of many to capture the kinetic motion of this great city, wrestling the fluidity of her canyons onto glass plates bathed in silver halides and gelatin, the latter being that vile byproduct obtained through the rendering of horses and cattle. ¶ This unlikely combination of slaughterhouse scrap and noble metal has, for well over a century and a half, acted as the intermediary between that which is fleeting and that which is still. ¶ I took to New York's streets with a fervor I had not previously known. Time and again I have found the newness of a place to be nearly intangible, the magic not abating, but becoming ever more elusive. In the city, however, as the honeymoon waned, the more truthful my relationship with her became. ¶ The vast majority of the photographs in this book were made between October 1987 and July 1990. Acting on both naiveté and a 25-year-old's sense of immortality, I uprooted from my native California and asked the city for harborage. I was consumed by photography and my passion was constantly fanned by my many influences, and an ever-growing awareness of what was possible with a camera. ¶

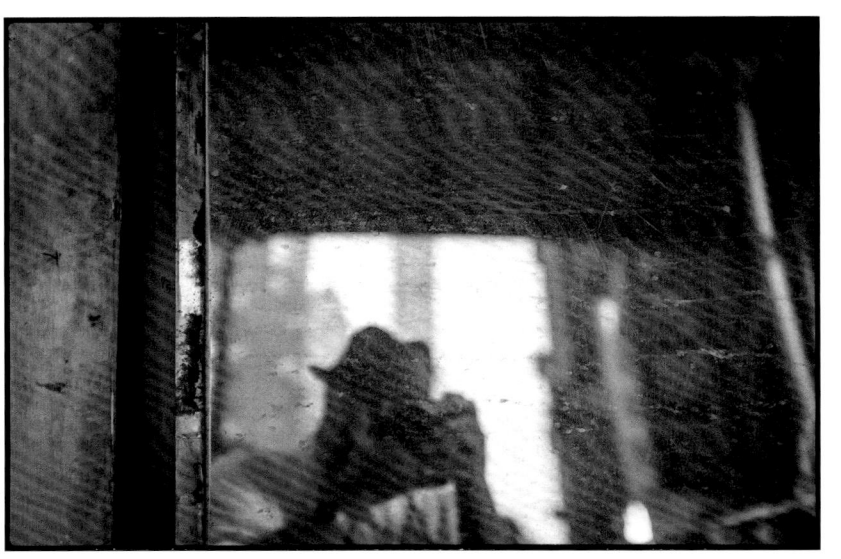

SPECIAL THANKS to my wife Kathryn and my son Dylan; you are always in my heart. Thank you Travis Smith for your integrity, skill, and devotion. Thank you Dave Yeager for your friendship and loyalty. Thank you to my dear friend Brett Kilroe for your kindness and love. To say you are missed would be an immense understatement. You are with me always. Thank you James Hughes for your friendship and help along the way. Thank you Ted Waitt for your support and insight. Thank you Andrew López for sharing your skill and passion. Thank you to my mentor John Gray. Your friendship over the years has meant everything to me. Thank you to Kevin Amer, Chris Callis, John Wells, Greg Heisler, Wendy Bryan, and Matt Mahurin for making my time in New York special.

THE
GREY
GHOST

The Grey Ghost:
New York City Photographs
1st Edition (1st printing, July 2016)
© 2016 Dan Winters
All images © Dan Winters

ART DIRECTION AND DESIGN
Andrew Massiatte López
and Dan Winters

DIGITAL PHOTO PRODUCTION
Travis Smith

EDITOR
Ted Waitt

PROJECT MANAGER
Lisa Brazieal

MARKETING MANAGER
Jessica Tiernan

ISBN
978-1-68198-083-6

Rocky Nook Inc.

1010 B Street, Suite 350
San Rafael, CA 94901 USA

rockynook.com

"*Sunken-Eyed Girl*"
Words and Music by Michael Doughty
Copyright © 2005 BMG Monarch and
Mc Monkey Twenty Seven Music

All Rights Administered by
BMG Rights Management (US) LLC
All Rights Reserved
Used by Permission

Reprinted by Permission of
Hal Leonard Corporation

Distributed in the U.S. by
Ingram Publisher Services

Distributed in the UK and Europe
by Publishers Group UK

Library of Congress
Control Number: 2015958930

Cover graphic by Travis Smith, based on the lobby mosaic of the Empire State Building. Original design by Leif Neandross, 1931.

FINAL PLATE
Dan Winters, Self Portrait, 6th Avenue, 2015.

Printed in Canada
This book is printed on acid-free paper.